HOME

THE RETURN TO WHAT YOU ALREADY ARE

CLARE DIMOND

Copyright © 2022 by Clare Dimond

All rights reserved.

No part of this book may be reproduced in any form or by any electronic or mechanical means, including information storage and retrieval systems, without written permission from the author, except for the use of brief quotations in a book review.

For everyone in the REAL community,

with sincere appreciation for the love and support you give each other.

FOREWORD

"Why are you so unhappy? Because 99% of everything you think and everything you do is for yourself. And there isn't one."

Wei Wu Wei

What you are about to read is liable to evoke your own destruction, but that's actually a good thing. Because the you that can be "destroyed" never really existed in the first place, like a character in a Shakespearian drama who dies at the end of Act V only to be born again six nights a week with a matinee performance on the weekend.

I first came across the ancient spiritual teaching most commonly known as "non-duality" while reading an interview with one of its more famous 20th century proponents, the Indian teacher Ramesh S. Balsekar. His teaching, at least as I heard it at the time, was that free will is an illusion and that everything in life is predetermined. Genocide was unavoidable, tragedy was written in the stars, and the struggles, stress, and disappointments of daily life just a part of the daily unfolding.

I thought it was the most depressing philosophy I'd ever come across.

Which is why I was so surprised by what happened next. Somewhere around page three of the interview, something in me began to relax and an almost indescribable glee rose up in me. If everything was predetermined, then all the pressure was off. I was free to simply live my life and see what happened without any need to control the outcome.

It was like reading an amazing story with me as the main character, unable to influence the plot but equally unable to stop reading as I eagerly awaited the revelation of each new twist and turn of the protagonist's fate. It was an experience of freedom I have never forgotten.

As my own story continued to unfold, I became enamoured of a metaphor that compared the self to an onion and suggested that the journey home to our true nature was as simple as peeling that onion until we got to its core.

So I bought an onion.

I took it to a park near my home in London, sat under what was the closest thing I could find to a Bodhi tree, and began to peel. Layer after layer came away and I grew more and more excited to see "my true nature", until the final layer of the onion fell away and I was left with... nothing. There was no core – no final piece – nothing left at all other than a small pile of onion peel in the paper bag that had once seemed to contain such promise. My disappointment was palpable. My true self was nothing and nowhere to be found.

FOREWORD

And then I looked up.

Suddenly, I was everything. I was the ground and the sky and the park. I was all of London and beyond. Like a wave looking down and recognising itself as the ocean out of which it arose, I was in that moment the punchline in the cosmic joke.

Both of those experiences – the utter freedom of losing all sense of free will and the sheer expansiveness of discovering that there's nothing solid at the core of an onion – make for good teaching stories. But the actual experience of home pointed to throughout this wonderful book is remarkably unremarkable.

You may have noticed the feeling of home during a particularly engaging project at work, while being overwhelmed by the beauty of a sunrise, or in the midst of a playful argument over who's going to hang up first after hours on the phone with a new friend.

It's in the sense of being part of something bigger than yourself while chanting with the crowd at a football match, and it's in losing all sense of a separate self while chanting "om shanti" to invoke peace at the end of a yoga class. In fact, in the words of one of Balsekar's teachers, the famed sage of Arunachala Ramana Maharshi, "We are always already home."

My first memory of Clare Dimond was of a young woman with shining eyes who asked to speak with me about what was causing her eyes to shine and how she could have more of whatever it was. Over the next year, she continued to shine while bravely navigating the challenges and possibilities we all encounter in our personal lives and professional ambitions.

FOREWORD

And then... lift off!

When our formal work together concluded, I got to stand back and watch her creative spark ignite as book after book emerged, each one packed with the wisdom of the ages and packaged in the wrapping paper of loving kindness.

I like to think that was all predetermined too, and that it couldn't have happened any other way. But in the end, all that matters is that it did happen.

And my fondest hope for you is that you find yourself on the pages of this book. Not the self you think you are and not the self you fear you might be, but rather the selfless self whose face you had before you were born.

With all my love,

Michael Neill

Best selling author of *The Inside Out Revolution* and *The Space Within*

HOME

PART I
INTRODUCTION

*Meanwhile the wild geese,
high in the clean blue air,
are heading home again.*
Mary Oliver

WELCOME HOME

Welcome back HOME.

(You have never gone away. It just might sometimes feel like you have.)

This is a book about what we really are and what the world really is.

What we are is Home. This is where what we really are always is.

And it is about the lived experience of not being Home. Of feeling alone, hopeless, scared, low, out of control, shameful, lacking. Lost.

And it is about how trying to find Home, from that place of lostness, makes the experience of lostness worse.

HOME is written to show that what we are is everything already.

That believed separation from what we really are, is the origin of all suffering.

The lived experience of what we are changes as mind, body, thoughts, beliefs, behaviour and understanding settle back Home.

Welcome back.

You've been here all along.

SIX 'POINTINGS'

*You believe that you live in the
universe when in reality the universe lives in you.*
Steve Chandler

My sister and I were in Costa one Sunday (we love a café). We were talking about holidays.

A memory came up of when we were in France in a swimming pool. I was waiting behind someone on the ladder to get out.

At the same time as I pulled myself up the ladder, the woman in front dipped down. Her foot went right down the top of my swimming costume.

In reality, it probably took less than a few seconds for her to extract her foot. In my memory it took so long that it is probably still there. My sister was next to us and saw the whole fee(t)asco.

In the cafe, my sister and I started laughing so hard remembering this that we just couldn't stop.

We were laughing and laughing and laughing and in the midst of laughing I caught her gaze and saw... what...?

What did I see in her eyes? What did she see in mine?

The laughter took away all veils and, in that moment, what was revealed?

Realness, truth, presence, Aliveness, joy, sameness, Love...

What remains when we look up at the night sky and all worries dissolve?

What creates that almost unconscious flow of movement, ideas, creation when we are absorbed in painting, writing, playing music, dancing, running, meditating?

What is perfectly moving the lungs and beating the heart even in our moments of feeling desperately incapable?

When we listen, what translates sound to meaning? When we speak, how do words form? When we dance, what moves our limbs?

What is unveiled when the miracle beauty of nature, a partner, a friend, a child, a pet takes our breath away?

What remains alert, alive and responsive while we sleep?

When we learn, what is making learning happen?

Through this book we will explore what that is.

We will consider what we are before the mind, before thought, before separation, before belief creates an idea of ourselves.

It is not easy to do this with words.

And there are many who would argue that it is impossible anyway. That words can never come close and the mind can never understand what lies before it.

However, what we are talking about here is logical and evident. It is impossible to argue with because, when the enquiring mind gets still with what is real, nothing else makes sense.

Different teachers use different words to point to what 'Home', the foundational truth of being, really is, .

There are different slants to these words, they point to different facets of beingness. In this book we are considering six of these different 'pointings' and what they indicate about who we are.

(I'm calling them 'pointings' because they cannot be described conceptually, the conscious mind built as it is from beliefs in separation must label and distinguish and cannot grasp the indivisible.)

For each of the 'pointings' we are considering what veils that truth, what keeps the mind in the experience that we are something other. And what allows the mind to settle into that truth.

All of them indicate the infinite and absolute.

The first is Consciousness or Awareness which is perhaps the 'pointing' most often described in spiritual teachings. We will consider how Consciousness cannot be an aspect of the individual mind, that it must precede thought and belief for thought and belief to even appear. That it must precede individuality and separation for the concepts of individuality and separation to even take form.

The second is Intelligence. We will consider ourselves as the Intelligence of life itself. We actually are the organising power. There is no separate 'me' with its own separate Intelligence. This has profound implications for our understanding of free-will, control and accountability.

The third is Aliveness or Life. In the moment of a person's death, what happens? The body is still there, exactly as it was when the person was alive. The clothes are the same, the hair, the features. But now the person is not there. So what is the person? The person cannot be the body. The person must be the life that animated the body and yet there is nothing personal about life. Even though this is what we are, the ultimate miracle of Aliveness is continually overlooked and forgotten. It is hidden continually by the illusory 'life and death' drama of the mind's creations.

The fourth is Wholeness. This is the essence of non-duality. There is no objectively separate thing and no objectively separate person which is why it has to be described by a non-defining term like 'non-duality'. Any other word would create of it a concept, a something. We'll look at what this makes clear about the material world and what we are.

The fifth is Peace. In this chapter we consider that true Peace is the knowing that the Intelligence of being will respond to whatever arises. That the true Peace of our being is unrelated to any external object or circumstance and nothing to do with any particular emotion or mental state. Peace is what lies prior to all experience.

And finally we consider Unconditional Love as our true nature. The mind knows that Love is our essence. It looks like we have to try to return Home by being loved. This sets us up for a lifetime of confusion until we realise that every interaction is revealing the futility of the search and the truth of us. No wonder we can suffer so much in our relationships with others and with ourselves.

For those readers who are already tuned into enquiry, you might use this book to consider 'pointings' that might not have resonated so much in the past. You have had a lot of experience in moving into this direction and now it can extend as a true space of exploration. With nothing to fix or secure and everything to experience, you are already open to seeing new possibilities and unknown worlds. For you, I hope the richness of truth starts to become more and more apparent.

And for those who are completely fresh to this, first of all, welcome. You are in exactly the right place. Begin by noticing the desire to have the right insight in order to create a different experience of life. Just notice that urge, and allow it to fall away into curiosity. Allow a real rigour to come to mind. Ask: is that true? Is what this book is saying really true? How could that be true? Use the inner sense, that comes from curiosity to see what resonates. And notice how the seeking energy, that desire to be something different, to feel something different negates enquiry. It keeps the mind trapped in its own resistance. Curiosity is the gateway to truth. And truth, as they say, sets us free.

This is a lifetime of the only exploration that makes any sense. What is true? What is real? What doesn't change?

Consciousness. Intelligence. Aliveness. Wholeness. Peace. Love.

Home.

Along with a great deal of laughter.

ILLUSION, RELATIVE AND ABSOLUTE WALK INTO A BAR

The notion of a separate organism is clearly an abstraction, as is also its boundary. Underlying all this is unbroken wholeness even though our civilisation has developed in such a way as to strongly emphasise the separation into parts.
David Bohm

I was on a first date, a drink in a pub as it happens, and of course he asked the question 'What do you do?'.

'I run programmes and write books that explore why there is no objective reality or separate self', I said.

'Isn't that a bit woo-woo?' he asked. (Which actually was an improvement on the 'Right…' and tumbleweed of another date I had.)

And I launched into a defence of what we are talking about in this book. The tension in my body clearly showed this was nothing to do with truth and everything to do with defending ME.

In that moment, my work had to be respected. He needed to understand. His view had to be corrected.

In other words, me, my, mine vs. he, him, his – all alive and well in a conversation about there being no objectively separate self and other... Let's face it – that wasn't going anywhere fast.

One of the biggest (and most valid criticisms) of a 'spiritual' approach is that it can lead to denial or bypass of reality. But on the other hand, when that reality looks so real that there is no space to see the greater truth, then that is also confusion.

So what is real? Was there really a Clare and a good-looking man in a pub (I'll preserve his anonymity poor fellow. It's already enough that he is featuring in a book after a two hour date)?

For the benefit of me on potential future dates and the purpose of this book, let's try to clear this up a bit. There were really three things going on in that conversation:

The Illusory

The Relative

The Absolute

Let's start (at the very beginning) with the Absolute.

This is what is beyond thought, beyond definition. It is what never changes, that has no limit or edge, that cannot be compared or judged or categorised.

As Michael Neill once said to me, it is like pointing to a fire with an icicle. The closer we get to it, the less we have to point with.

Nevertheless, the Absolute exists, (indeed is the only thing that is) and is what gives rise to and creates the experience of life in form.

This is Home. The Absolute. Ultimately it is what we are.

Teachers and authors put words to the Absolute knowing that these are only a half way house to describing the indescribable. (Hence the term 'non-dual', describing what it is by saying what it isn't).

Nevertheless, words are all we have in a book and they can go some way at least to a sense of what we are and what we are not.

This book is dedicated to exploring some of the most intriguing descriptors of this infinite, absolute space:

'Consciousness' (Part 2)

'Intelligence' (Part 3)

'Aliveness' (Part 4)

'Wholeness' (Part 5)

Peace (Part 6) and

Love (Part 7).

All of which are infinite, Absolute and fundamentally what we are. Without this, no us. And, it could be said, without us - a sensory form with experiential capacity, no glimpse even of this.

The Absolute is deepest Peace because it is the only truth. It is the deepest freedom, because the truth sets us free.

The reality of that evening in the pub is that the Absolute was the only objective, reliable truth. There was Consciousness, Aliveness, Intelligence. Unchanging. Unaffected. Impossible to distort.

And this whole truth and only truth was momentarily obscured in that mini fight for survival of defending my work. 'My' identity was under-threat. When it looks like the identity is us, this is life and death. Stress, tension, conflict.

And all because the Absolute was hidden by the drama of the story of me.

Which opens up the very valid questions 'But what about Hitler? What about violence and poverty? What about cancer? What about pain? What about grief and death of loved ones?'

Are you saying none of that is real...?

Right. Looks like it is time now to move on to the Relative...

The worst that happened to me in that pub was a man saying my work was a bit woo-woo. But what if he had stolen my wallet? Or hit me? Or drugged and kidnapped me?

If we say none of that is real, that it's all just 'a story of me' or a 'dream' aren't we heading into the very dangerous area of hands over the ears, tra-la-la-la spiritual bypass?

Absolutely we are (see what I did there?)

And this is a pivotal point in this exploration: the recognition of the Relative.

This is the world of apparent form. Tables, chairs, this body, other bodies, pints of beer, fish and chips... (just using what was in the pub as an example. There are many other forms of course. Pints of cider for example. Scampi and chips. Pie and chips. Sausage and chips... Endless...)

The word 'apparent' is important. Because these objects are perceived (unlike the Absolute, which enables perception and is therefore prior to all appearances). And perception, of course, is a distorting tool.

Sensory limits cut off a potential reality which exists but which isn't available to the perceiving organism. The labrador dog in the corner with its approximately 300 million scent glands would be experiencing a world of aromas that did not exist for me and my date (maximum 10 million scent glands between us). And the experience of the organism subconsciously dictates the appearance, meaning, associations, implications, category, definition, storage of that perception.

So all 'objects' are Relative. Appearance is not Absolute. The material world has to exist in perception. It cannot exist any other way.

And yet it still has an apparent reality to it, the denial of which serves no one.

Problems arise in the human world because of the tremendously powerful, creative spin the mind puts on simple apparent reality. We are not just dealing with the actual real time data available in this moment. We are dealing with all the meanings, associations, memories, imagined futures. None of which are Absolute truth yet the on-going experience of the world appears objectively, independently and concretely real.

These problems aren't solved by denial (which only makes them more apparently real, just now they are things that can't be talked about). They are solved or rather dis-solved through presence, openness to reality, enquiry and healing of the projected conditioning and trauma that turns reality into a war zone.

All of this takes us, finally, to the illusory...

The thing that looks more real than anything else, the thing that plays the starring role of all drama, all stories, all experiences, all conflicts, all problems: the separate self.

How ironic it is that the thing that is unquestioned, that is defended, obsessed about, focused on, promoted, protected doesn't actually exist.

And by 'separate self', what I mean here, is the idea of a separate, independent, objectively perceiving, behaviour-controlling me. An entity of self-hood that is believed to be operating the body, making decisions, doing the actions. A 'me' that is somehow a separate chess piece, its own independent manager of life, Consciousness, Intelligence.

That's the me that does not exist. That me is 100% illusory. And yet it is the thing that looks most real of all.

Defending that 'me' in the pub was physical, emotional and intellectual. It was conscious and sub-conscious. It linked back in that moment to every experience of being dismissed or not taken seriously. It vibrated in the need to be heard, admired and secure. It needed to survive and it equated survival with approval.

And yet, what is that me?

The only truth of us is the Absolute, momentarily located in Relative temporary, perception-created, sensory form.

The collection of hurts, knocks, trauma, resentments, vigilance, defence mechanisms that form the identity has neither an

Absolute or a Relative truth. The past exists as a construction of this moment. So does the identity. As understanding shifts, as healing happens, the entirety of that old self disappears.

This is enlightenment. And it is also death in one sense. The death of an idea of what we are that has been clung to at all cost. Which is why the thought of the separate self idea disappearing might feel tremendously confronting. It's OK though. YOU, as you really are - are not disappearing in any way. In fact the experience of being you will only become more stable, reliable, healthy and sane.

True enlightenment is the on-going healing of those shames, fears and insecurities that create the logical, understandable, innocent but ultimately problematic need to control and defend an identity of ourselves as separate from the whole.

And this is the focus of HOME. How the illusory ego can be understood for what it is. How beliefs, even those held for decades dissolve into the only truth of the Absolute. How, this process of dissolution opens up a greater intimacy, reality and sanity with the world of apparent form.

So in conclusion…

There was a man and a woman in a pub.

Albeit they existed only as a Relative appearance in the experience of anyone or thing that perceived them.

The man was a creation of the woman.

The woman was a creation of the man.

Both were a creation of the perceptions of others in the bar.

The labrador's perception of them was probably an aroma overload of first date deodorants, aftershaves, perfumes…

This is the Relative. We exist, in any particular form, in perception.

However, the entire ever-changing experience of self and other was only possible because of the never-changing Absolute.

Consciousness was bringing into awareness the experience of all of this.

Intelligence was creating, from visual, auditory and sensory data, images, sounds and perceptions.

Aliveness was animating the bodies, making perception possible.

This is the Absolute.

And that separate self identity – the spider in the web which obscures the Absolute and which makes of the Relative a fixed reality that has to be resisted and controlled...?

Only ever the Illusion.

Woo-woo?

Yes of course it is.

Spine-tinglingly, hair-on-back-of-neck-raising. Yes. Mind-blowingly so.

And yet this is reality, this is all there is.

Profoundly peaceful.

Yet as basic, prosaic, familiar, fundamental and every-day as it is possible to get.

A bit like Home, really.

ZOOMING IN AND OUT

*Our greatest contribution to humanity
is our awakening.
It is to literally leave the state of consciousness that the mass of
humanity is in and discover the truth of our being, which is the
truth of all beings.*
Adyashanti

When we're driving along my son loves to play with the zoom in and out function on the sat nav. Moving all the way out – street, town, country, continent until the blue and green world appears in space. And then all the way back – world, continent, country, town, street, house.

It's interesting the zoom in and out function. Especially when it comes to the Intelligence of life and how it appears within the reality of the self, the mind, the body and a world of other people, objects and forms.

And it's rather ironic that the one thing that, from a certain view point, looks absolutely real, which grabs all the attention and which looks to be the source and owner of Intelligence and information for navigating life (in other words, the deciding, separate individual self) – is one hundred per cent illusory.

Because zooming in to see what the self-identity really is reveals belief after belief, assumption after assumption, learned reaction after learned reaction... and nothing else.

Open attention on what is true about what we think we are inevitably reveals the illusion. The idea of ourselves as an entity separate from life, from Consciousness cannot withstand scrutiny. It disappears as soon as it is genuinely investigated. There is no logic to it.

It has no mechanics, no physics, no biology of its own – even though the belief in the self can affect how all of this appears and is experienced. No substance or endurance. It is belief based and beliefs cannot survive enquiry.

As this idea of a controlling, deciding, individual self dissolves, there is no longer a focus on that illusion (not least because it's not there...).

All the energy taken up in the impossible task of securing the identity, controlling its behaviour and environment is now freed up for zooming in to what is actually here.

And what is actually here is still Intelligence animating and orientating a world of apparent form.

Look around the room you are in.

Maybe it has a chair, a table. Maybe there are other people in the room. There is certainly 'your' body.

They look absolutely real. And yet they are not objective truths. They are not a fixed reality. Everything about the way they appear and are held in the mind is a creation and agreement of perception, learning and conditioning.

The zooming in allows all these objects to be understood for what they really are.

However, the difference between these apparent objects and the self-identity is that while, on investigation, the 'separate self' disappears, these objects do not. With open enquiry, they become a richer, more extraordinary next layer of themselves.

The zooming in to the world of apparent form continues to reveal more and more information.

Objects (including the body), become more and more true with curious attention. They are the gateway to infinite information about the material world, its agreements, its possibilities, its seamlessness, expanding knowledge and capability beyond what could ever have been imagined.

This means that, as we zoom into truth, two things happen:

Firstly, the mind-body becomes more aligned to reality (i.e. sane) because there is less fighting against and attempts to secure what doesn't exist.

Secondly, we become more able to function in the world because objects are no longer viewed through the confusion of the distorting, identified, believing mind. They are freed up to be what they really are: placeholders of potential, containers of information.

This of course is a logical irony in its own right.

The less real the self-identity appears, the more freedom there is for expression and exploration.

The less fixed the world appears, the more intimacy, freedom and possibility within it.

Zooming into the human system must mark the end of self-improvement. There is no self to 'improve'. Nothing is personal. The identity is a confusion. The idea that there is an individual deciding self is impossible to sustain.

And it marks the start of the clearest and deepest possible learning about the body, its behaviours and the world. It is a fresh understanding of what life is, of what form is, of what objects are, of mechanics, physics, biology and chemistry, of space and relationships between objects, of where actions come from and their impact.

We zoom in and in, getting closer to the truth with each click of the dial. Assumptions fall away, centuries old 'realities' are disproved, meanings dissolve, identification ends.

And from that only true place of potential in form, we can zoom out again, out and out, the frame revealing more and more. Zooming out until the whole world, the universe, everything, is there, held in our view, contained within us. It is clear what we are. What truth is.

From this greatest of all perspectives, the whole universe contained within us, we can go back in, back into the world of form. Zooming in to the tiniest details. The angle of a spoon in a coffee cup. The surface tension of a tear drop. The breath of a tree on our skin.

Zooming into the detail reveals the truth, the miracle in the way that a fraction-of-a-second locking of eyes conveys the whole world.

Zooming out beyond the detail reveals the truth, the infinite and absolute in which the details appear and disappear.

A world of truth setting itself free.

The ultimate navigation system.

All roads pointing Home.

PART II
CONSCIOUSNESS

We're not human beings having a spiritual experience. We're one spiritual being having seven billion human experiences. And who you really are is that one spiritual being. Your true identity is consciousness itself.
Teilhard de Chardins

The chicken and the egg were, once again, having their eternal argument.

'Chickens come first' said the chicken. 'Obviously they do. They have to be here for eggs to exist.'

'You're wrong,' said the egg. 'Obviously without eggs - no chickens. Eggs first.'

This went on and on and on for millennia until the farmer fed up with all the arguing came over to them.

'Farmer' they said, 'Please settle this once and for all. Which came first - chicken or egg?.'

The farmer sat down on a bale of hay and thought for a moment.

'Well chicken,' he began, 'where does the egg appear for you?'

'Over there' said the chicken, pointing to the egg.

'Yes' agreed the farmer, 'But what actually experiences the egg?'

'My brain?' asked the chicken.

'And what experiences your brain?'

The chicken thought for a moment and said hesitantly, 'Umm my consciousness. I guess."

'And where does the idea of you appear?' he asked.

'Same place…. in my consciousness' said the chicken.

'Which comes first, then, the idea of 'me and my' or consciousness?' asked the farmer.

'It must be consciousness' replied the chicken.

The farmer turned to the egg and asked the same questions about where the chicken appeared. The egg ended ultimately with the same answer.

'Without consciousness would you exist in the way you appear to?' he asked them both.

They looked at each other. 'No…'

'So what does that mean you both are?'

'Consciousness…'

'And so just to clear it up 100%', concluded the farmer, 'because we all know this has been going on for *quite* some time… what came first? Chicken, egg or…'

'Consciousness' they both replied.

'Job done' said the farmer, and, having drawn a line under an entire genre of joke, went back to his work.

WE ARE CONSCIOUSNESS

Whatever you think this world is, whatever you think you are, and whatever you think of anything in this world is your ego. And anyone who surpasses that, that is called the death of the ego. And that world, before time, space and matter is pure unadulterated consciousness.

Sydney Banks

One evening, I was on my own watching *'Fleabag'*, the series created by Phoebe Waller-Bridge. Fleabag is the main character (we never learn her real name).

Her sister in the programme is called Claire. Married to someone who treats her appallingly, Claire is in love with a Scandinavian man she has met through her work. He is called Klare.

Fleabag and her sister bump into this man in the park. (It's the 'I look like a pencil!' haircut scene for those in the know.)

The scene ends with Fleabag firstly turning to her sister and saying "Bye Claire".

Then she turns to the man and says, "Bye Klare…

…And *then she turns to the camera (ie to ME the viewer!!!) and says "Bye Clare".*

Yikes! I almost jumped out of my skin. (My name is Clare remember. It might not have had the same effect if my name was anything else). For a split second I felt like I'd crossed a line between two dimensions, suspended between two planets, in two worlds simultaneously.

Because, as absolutely involving, moving and engaging as a piece of film is, the characters on screen exist in a different (unreal) plane to the viewer, the (real) conscious space in which they appear.

The characters in the film and the viewer of the film do not exist in the same reality.

While the viewer is engaged in the film, however, it looks absolutely real. In those moments, the viewer is oblivious to the fact that it is just a creation.

The viewer is fully identified in to the movie, moved by the drama, engaged in the twists and turns of the relationships.

The viewer's only actual reality, as witness, as the space in which all elements of the movie arise, is forgotten about.

And then something breaks the spell of identification with the movie.

It might get boring. It might be a bit of bad acting or clunky script. It might be the Starbucks cup in the Game of Thrones. It might be someone coming into the living room and asking if we want a cup of tea. It might be the closing music beginning and the end credits appearing.

(It probably won't be one of the characters apparently turning to you and addressing you by name, I'm afraid. That is reserved only for very special people.)

Without the viewer in the first place though, the programme could not have been experienced. It could not exist in the way it appears to.

Consciousness is the first 'pointing' of this book. Consciousness is the viewer. It is the illuminated present in which everything happens and of which everything is made. Without Consciousness there would be nothing, no-thing, nothing visible, nothing sensed, nothing felt, nothing seen or heard.

Consciousness is the prerequisite to anything appearing, in the way that a viewer is the prerequisite to the film being seen, to the film coming into existence.

The film is so vivid, so real, so gripping, so enthralling that the fact of the viewer is completely disregarded. The act of viewing is irrelevant (even though, in reality, it is the only truth). The film is grabbing all attention.

But what is the film? What is it made of? It is fascinating to consider that, while that film, that arc of tragedy and drama and adventure and tension and loss, appears so compellingly, objectively real, it is actually made of the viewer.

In a conversation about reality, what becomes clear is that the thing that looks so real, the film, does not exist as anything tangible or real. It is the viewing, that is making it all possible.

When the film, that drama, that tension starts to become less compelling, it starts to be recognised for what it is, a creation of Consciousness.

It becomes recognised that that is what we are. And that is mind-blowing. The mind begins to settle back into the truth that all these comings and goings are happening *within* awareness. Without Consciousness or awareness, nothing.

We can explore the idea of Consciousness a bit more deeply with the dream analogy. When we are asleep, we might dream of a 'me' character going through different experiences and endeavours. That entire set up is happening within the existence of the dreamer. The character in the dream, as real as it looks, as much like us as it appears, is just a creation of mind in that moment, made possible because there is a dreamer.

The dream is made possible by the dreamer and the dream is made of the dreamer: it is all the same thing. There is no possibility of separating dream and dreamer. There is not even any possibility of separating anything within the dream, as much as it appears that it is a real world, that there are real people and real events, it is still a creation of the dream.

Within the dream, it looks like survival can only be achieved through controlling the happenings *within the dream* and that safety is only possible by securing the character. But actually, because the whole thing is taking place within the dreamer's sleeping mind, the only possible solution for that character is for the dreamer to wake up. In other words, the only way the character's challenges can end is for the dream to end and the character to disappear. On waking, there is no character, no threat.

HOME

What we start to see from this, is that the Consciousness that we are enables an experience of a separate idea of what we are. But the truth is that we are only that space in which that lived experience of separation arises.

Through this section of HOME we are essentially considering this shift of lived experience:

From a human conscious mind identified in to the drama, believing its beliefs…

…To a human conscious mind that is no longer identified to the drama and is settling back into its truth as the viewer, the dreamer, the Consciousness space in which everything appears.

When we suffer, the mind is trying to find its way within the dream back to reality, to Wholeness but it can never achieve that. The dream depends on the belief that it is real, and that it is separate from the dreamer, separate from the Consciousness that we are.

Trying to find our way Home within the dream only maintains the dream further.

Isn't that right, Claire?

Klare?

Clare…?

HOW CONSCIOUSNESS IS VEILED

If you were an all-powerful, all-knowing consciousness, you could never know sadness, loss, anxiety, surprise, or the excitement of not knowing what will happen next. An all-knowing consciousness could not enjoy jokes or cry at tragedies. By playing the game, consciousness delights in every experience possible, and the only way to do that is for it to lose itself in us.
Chris Niebauer

I expect we've all had nightmares. A regular one I had as a child (brought on by the hallucinogenic strength of late 1970s nit lotion) was of being chased. I don't know by what but it was terrifying. In the dream I was like a parkour ninja 40 years ahead of her time, leaping across rivers, jumping from windows and scaling walls to get away.

The reason they were nightmares is, of course, because they looked true. Within the nightmare, the character (me) or things that the character needs or loves are under threat.

There are rules within the nightmare and, within those rules, the character has to somehow find safety.

That dream is so utterly absorbing because it looks absolutely real.

And what makes it look real is the tension it contains. There is the grip of emotion. It looks to be life and death. The 'me' that is only ever a representation, an avatar, a believed idea is under threat. Survival is at stake.

"That's all very well, Clare," you might say. 'But you are talking about dreams and nightmares. (And in the previous chapter, tv programmes and films.). This has got nothing to do with real life and real problems with real people, real jobs, real money, real economies, real illnesses, real houses, real events…"

It is confronting to hear it, but as it is when we are asleep in bed, so it is when we are going about our daily life in the tension, stress, resistance and defence of an identity under threat.

The infinite and absolute Consciousness that we really are has become illusorily condensed into the self identity or idea. And it looks that what we are can be threatened, troubled or extinguished.

This attention-grabbing fight for survival of the dream character blanks out the truth of the dreamer.

We are not talking about actual physical survival. We are talking about the survival of the image of ourselves. The image that is created from conditioned learning about what we are and what we need to be. The threat to this image is often perceived as more serious than threat to the physical body.

It is why people say they would rather die than speak in public.

Or why we can feel actual physical pain on being rejected.

It is why humiliation, embarrassment and failure can create such intense reactions and avoidance behaviour.

It is why, once rejection, lack, worthlessness and isolation have been learned, they can become the overlay to our reality even when it is not really there.

It is why the idea of a future (which is only ever imagination) can create panic and anxiety.

And why the idea of the past (which exists as it is experienced right now) can create depression.

All of these revolve around an idea of ourselves that must be protected and a projected view of what other people think and of what will happen. The mind, in these moments, is trying to find stability on the turbulent sea of thought, belief and conditioning.

When there is an immediate risk of physical harm, however, no thoughts of identity, past or future are relevant.

The threat to the survival of the actual body means all attention and resources, are in that moment, focused on reality. All resistance to 'what is' is released to allow access to real, physical body-preserving data.

Everything that is not actually real and of use - all future anxiety and past depression, all insecurity, all comparisons - goes out of the window as all attention is dedicated to this immediate reality and its danger, right now.

HOME

The vulnerability of the character in the dream is not survival of the physical. It is the survival of a 'me' that appears separate and objectively real.

And that is the greatest veil, the ultimate obscuring. The identity, the fear, the insecurity can be torture. The grip of it is overwhelming. It blocks out everything else and we are right there in the film. The buttons and triggers in our life transport the entire knowing of existence into this fixed apparent reality and its fight for survival.

The tension is obscuring the Consciousness that makes it all possible in the first place. That is where the mind gets lost inside a view of the world that is dictated by what has been learned, by our identity, by our shame, fear and insecurity.

It is battling within the dream to find safety but it never will find it. Because the only experience of true safety is the realisation that we are the dreamer. Where has the dream gone on waking? Nowhere. It was never really there in the first place.

In the dream, the conscious human mind is identified with the personal. It fully believes (and simultaneously resists) its own narration.

We have grown up in environments in which the belief in the self identify as a separate controlling entity is ubiquitous and unquestioned. From the moment we are first praised or blamed or worse, a powerful conditioning process is in place.

And when the lived experience of what we are (inevitably) suffers within this, the self-help guides and the therapies and the drugs so often send us down the route of trying to be better, trying to control emotions or else masking and numbing all the way.

The industry to 'switch off the self', in other words, numb this identification, silence the 'selfing' voice and control emotions is now worth $4 trillion a year according to Steven Kotler and Jamie Wheal in their book *Stealing Fire*. Alcohol, drugs, food, sex, gambling etc are used to mask the suffering of separation but, as we all know, only increase it over time.

Fortunately for all of us, this does not have to continue. Too much is known now about the truth of the human mind for that wild goose chase of searching for Peace and happiness within the unquestioned belief system of separation to continue.

It is now 2022 and —marvel upon marvels—the 'Nitty Gritty Nit Free Comb' has been invented. Not even a drop of lotion is required to rid my children's hair of unwelcome guests.

Now, if the human species is intelligent enough to invent such a miracle device as that…

then surely…

surely…

it is ready to come back to its (nit-free, nightmare-free) Home.

HOW CONSCIOUSNESS IS REVEALED

It could be said that understanding is the intellectual aspect of consciousness, love is the feeling aspect of consciousness, and beauty is the perceptual aspect of consciousness.
Francis Lucille

It didn't matter how many windows I jumped from, rivers I leapt or walls I scaled. There was no safety in the dream. Anywhere. The dream itself was a danger creating mechanism. Solve one problem and immediately another arose. This is thought and mind created. There is no limit on what can be conjured up within it.

How could I find safety in those nightmares of mine?

Only by waking up.

On waking up, although there might still be the residues of tension left in the body, it was obvious that the Clare in danger was only a character.

The dissolution of the dream itself is the 'escape'. And in the 'escape' it is clear there is nothing to escape from. It is realised that whether I wake up or not, I'm safe because the dream me is not what I am.

But the lived experience of a nightmare, of course, is horrible.

And it is the same in our daily lives. The lived experience of fear, insecurity, shame and need projected as a believed self and reality creates tremendous suffering.

What brings the experience of what we are back to the space that is simultaneously observing and creating everything it observes?

What would shift the experience of ourselves into that witnessing space of no identification, no judgement, no labelling, no sense even of any meaning or differentiation, no fight and flight?

The key shift is the conscious mind.

Through this exploration, that identified, believer's conscious mind is shown again and again to be a product of conditioned programming. The idea of ourselves as separate (in other words the dream character) is a learned idea.

Through these realisations, the conscious mind is freed from the programme and settles into what is actually true: the witnessing presence, awareness and Consciousness that it really is. This is a neutral space. It contains no beliefs. It is simply the space in which everything arises.

This is healing.

It is the dissolution of the survival fear, traumas and shocks that are layered into the embodied experience of what we are.

And so the healing, this shift from identified mind to the truth of pure Consciousness, must begin with the body.

The body is as proximate and as pure as it is possible to get to reality. Attention can rest on the actual simplest sensations prior to any labelling, meaning or resistance. This is the truest possible meeting of 'formless' and 'form', of Absolute and Relative.

There are sensations in the body that must be felt to be released.

And it begins with noticing whatever is being felt within the body right now.

What is that sensation? Attention can go deeper into the muscles, the tendons, the cells even. As the focus goes deeper within, it moves through the layers of interpretations, thoughts of the past, the future, all the way through to purest observation of sensation.

This is not even about feelings or emotions, because a feeling is already an act of labelling, with implicit judgement. We are interested now in just the purest sensation.

And this can be done at any moment, in any situation. Whenever there is a contraction. A moment of separation. A me and a them. A moment of resistance or seeking or judgement. A barrier coming up. A fight or flight movement.

In these moments, all attention can turn in towards the discomfort. Feeling it in the body. Witnessing what the mind is creating.

This brings the system, and attention into reality.

It allows the mind to settle down through all those levels of interpretation. Just through to simple observation.

This is powerful because it is the opposite of what has been happening all our lives. We have done everything possible to avoid the physical sensations while placing all attention on that narrative of separation in the conscious mind. Now that is being reversed. The reality is the sensations. That is all there is. The mind's story has no truth.

This practice of witnessing the sensations is not about getting rid of them. In fact it is the opposite, it is about having the absolute fullness of them. Allowing them, welcoming them, loving them, honouring them.

In that space it becomes clear that there is no differentiation between the sensation observed and the observer. There is no separate thing. The observation and the thing are both made of observation, made of Consciousness.

This is a profound realisation that starts to shift all experience back to its source. It starts to shift the entire activity of mind into the open, infinite space in which everything arises.

The mind is set free. It now can fulfil its rightful role. Of creativity, conceptualisation, planning, imagining, projecting. All without any of it being believed, identified with as personal and then resisted.

No longer believed. Just noticed.

No longer a never-ending fight with its own reflection. Just a creative resource.

Our practice, perhaps for the rest of our lives, is to shift from that separating, defining, labelling mind as the believed reality to the observation space in which the purest sensations can be had until it becomes clear that observation and observed are the same.

Ultimately, our true nature of Consciousness is revealed by the realisation that the personal is not the truth.

The drama and tension of the personal story becomes less exciting than the marvel of Consciousness, of being the source of all appearance.

And of course, Consciousness doesn't have to be revealed. It makes no difference. Whether it is realised that that is what we are or not, Consciousness remains the same.

The suffering and lostness of the experience of self can be seen for what it is.

The dream is understood.

The mind settles back Home.

IN SUMMARY….

Consciousness…

WHAT IS IT?

The pre-requisite to all appearance, all experience, all lived idea of self and the world.

The viewing, witnessing space of awareness.

The screen on which the film plays out.

The dreamer in which the dream is taking place.

WHAT VEILS IT?

The conscious mind becoming absorbed in the content of experience.

Identification with the content (that experience believed to be *what I am*) rather than the witnessing of the content.

Unquestioned belief that what is experienced is reality.

WHAT REVEALS IT?

Beliefs falling away because they are obviously not true.

The ending of identification with the transient and ever-changing.

A greater capacity to sit with discomfort as experience shifts from the imagined to simple reality.

The conscious mind increasingly settling into its truth as the witnesser of all appearance.

PART III
INTELLIGENCE

I go down to the shore in the morning
and depending on the hour the waves
are rolling in or moving out,
and I say, oh, I am miserable,
what shall–
what should I do? And the sea says
in its lovely voice:
Excuse me, I have work to do.
Mary Oliver

Once upon a time, all the animals and plants in the forest were getting into a debate about who was the best.

'I have the sharpest vision. So I must be the best.' said the hawk.

'Who cares?' said the rose, 'I am the most beautiful'

'I have the most powerful hearing' said the bat.

'Well I am the most abundant' said the moss.

'I am the most fragrant' said the lavender

'I am the largest' said the old oak tree.

It went on for weeks until eventually they decided to ask the old woman in the small house in the middle of the forest to decide it for them.

She stood in the clearing. They all waited.

'Hawk' she began, 'How is it that you see so well? How do your eyes focus so sharply? How do they track even the slightest movement?'

'I don't know', said the hawk. 'That's just what my eyes do. Seeing just happens.'

'Rose' she continued. 'How are you making yourself so beautiful? How are you growing those petals in those stunning patterns and in that marvellous range of hues and tones?'

'I don't know,' said the rose. 'The petals just grow.'

The woman continued. 'Bat, how do you hear sounds?'

'Well…' said the bat. 'Something in me creates waves of sound. I don't know how. My ears work out location when the sounds bounce back. I don't know how I do that either. Hearing just happens.'

And so it went on, through hundreds of thousands of creatures and plants. Each one realising they did not know what actually gave rise to their features and abilities.

When the last had spoken, they watched the woman, waiting for her to proclaim the winner.

Instead, she was gazing into the distance.

It took a long time for her to speak and, when she did, it was so quiet, almost under her breath and she only said three words. They weren't even her words.

'It just happens.'

They looked around at each other, taking in the remarkable, spectacular, incredible differences. The colours, the sizes, the shapes, the talents, the sounds, the qualities, the skills…

Differences which had revealed ultimately… well… no difference at all.

The debate was settled.

WE ARE INTELLIGENCE

That is unquestionably the most astounding thing about us—that we are just a collection of inert components, the same stuff you would find in a pile of dirt... the only thing special about the elements that make you is that they make you. That is the miracle of life.
Bill Bryson

An ape remembers a tool they need to retrieve an inaccessible reward and heads off in search of it.

A cave man sketches a hunt scene on the stone wall, allowing for the transportation of his learning to another, long after the hunt itself is over.

A scientist designs a rocket that will reach a planet no one has never visited.

Even the amoeba, a single-celled organism, stores memory in protein structures.

All of this made possible by Intelligence in form.

In this section we are looking at the infinite organising Intelligence of life.

There are trillions of cells in the human body and, within each, a nucleus is sending directions to the cell to grow, mature, divide, or die. This Intelligence in action at a microscopic cellular level becomes more complex and organised as the cells form tissue, organs, organ systems and eventually the human organism.

What is this Intelligence? It is a dynamic, coordinated, organising force. It is not be confused with the intellect which is the faculty of reasoning and understanding. The faculty of the intellect depends wholly on the Intelligence of life to exist. Without the fundamental Intelligence, seamlessly and continually integrating, responding, calibrating, balancing… nothing.

And without form, the organising power of life cannot appear. Information is Intelligence in form. The forms might appear to be separate - apes, cavemen, scientists, amoebas - but the organising Intelligence of which they are made is indivisible.

The more evolved and complex the organism, the greater the ability to take information and move conceptually, intellectually and experientially beyond immediate reality as it is right now.

As far as we know, humans are the only species able to explore and conceptualise the Intelligence that brings them into existence.

And modern humans are, of course, extremely able in this regard. (It is simultaneously our greatest advantage and our greatest disadvantage.)

Let's look closely at what is going on.

The brain, perception, emotion and behaviour combination is a dynamic learning system, created, maintained and animated by life Intelligence.

It continually responds to stimuli and environmental changes in order to maintain the survival of the organism.

Learning is 'packaged' up as a concept or as a representation, applied in other situations, shared or future-cast.

This is an enormous advantage. In the child, learning is taking place that the cup, once dropped, will always fall downwards and that learning is applied to other objects, other situations, other times.

We say 'the child is learning how cups fall'. Or 'I am learning to drive' or 'I am learning French' but that process of learning - how words, actions and phenomena are actually converted into rules, responses and expectations - is not governed by the conscious mind. The 'I' I believe I am has nothing to do with how learning actually happens.

This packaging of learning is efficient and practical. Depending on how complex the organism, the greater the wealth of information that can be managed.

Because mental phenomena create a limitless world of infinite potential, they allow for language and communication, planning and references to events that happened a second or millennia ago, future projections, scientific discoveries, art and literature, buildings and creations…

Where human problems begin is when these packaged up concepts become embedded as beliefs and unquestioned ways of perceiving and responding that are dysfunctional and tenacious.

Instead of (as happens in the amoeba) a construct dissolving in the face of new information, it now has a longevity to it. It becomes the lens through which reality is viewed. This distorting lens filters out anything that doesn't support the belief and focuses in on anything that provides more evidence for it.

The distortion confirms, maintains and intensifies itself.

So the once-upon-a-time learned version of self, other and reality becomes the all-the-time version.

That same child-brain creating unconscious mental rules about gravity and objects, might also be forming the concept that the child has to cry to get food or be invisible to avoid abuse or be charming to get attention. Or anything else. And these beliefs will remain, dynamically creating experience, until they no longer look true.

The reality we experience therefore is not reality. It is the experience of the embedded and embodied mental phenomena. Our lives are the on-going continuation of what was once learned. Often to the extent of serious harm to self and other.

Mental phenomena, conscious and unconscious, when misunderstood, trap lived experience, in a learned version of reality which, at best, is a waste of time, energy and resources and at worst risks the very survival of the individual itself, other people and their environment.

The amoeba does not have this problem. Its primitive protein memory structures dissolve and reform rapidly in response to environmental changes. The simplicity of its structure, its continual 'now-ness' mean that its reactions and behaviours are never stuck in a created version of itself and reality.

The human, on the other hand, is a different kettle of fish (so to speak). We can have all sorts of behavioural tendencies, emotional patterns or prolonged mental states that originated in response to a past reality but which are to the detriment of the life we are living now.

It might be habits around food, health, money, sex, socialising, gambling, drugs. It might be feelings of depression, anxiety, insecurity, fear, shame, jealousy... It might be tendencies towards conflict, numbing, distraction, comparison, withdrawal...

We try to change these, in other words we try to un-learn an old way of being or re-learn a new way. And, more often than not, we fail. We remain stuck in these patterns, habits and addictions. Why is that? Why can we not, like the amoeba, instantly dissolve and recreate our mental, physical and behavioural phenomena?

Because there has been no change in the apparent reality.

No aspect of reality is objectively true in the way it appears to be, *but the self concept, entirely made of thought and belief, is less true than anything else*. Unlike the cup or the child's body it has no apparent form. Unlike gravity it has no consistency or applicability.

The unquestioned self concept is the original distorting lens. The self's attempt to try to change itself and the world is conditioning trying to change conditioning, a belief trying to change a belief, the unreal trying to change the unreal.

It can probably go without saying that we cannot un-learn or re-learn anything in relation to ourselves while the concept of ourself is taken as fixed reality.

Change happens from the understanding that mental phenomena – conscious or unconscious – are constructions not reality. And that the self construct is the least real of all.

The amoeba, even though it has the presence and purity of response that even the most non-dual of gurus can only hope for, is, of course, not the aim for us.

That would be regression. It makes no sense, even if it were possible, to dissolve our remarkable human mental capacities.

The pinnacle is (as pointed out by Maslow, in a later edition to his triangle): self transcendence.

The movement through and beyond the unreal, but tenaciously believable, concept of a defined, separate, objective, individual self.

The freedom of living, with all the advantages of the super-powered human mind understood for what they are.

The unlimited potential of being infinite and absolute life Intelligence in human form.

HOW INTELLIGENCE IS VEILED

I know this world is ruled by infinite intelligence. Everything that surrounds us- everything that exists - proves that there are infinite laws behind it. There can be no denying this fact. It is mathematical in its precision.
Thomas A. Edison

*L*et's do an experiment to kick off this section on how Intelligence is veiled.

Close your mouth. (That sounds rude. It's not meant to be. I just don't have a more polite way of saying it. Oh wait…)

Please close your mouth.

Let the tongue rest with the tip against the lower front teeth.

And with the mouth remaining closed, say the vowel sounds of the English language one by one.

A

E

I

O

U

(If you now have that 1983 song by Freez, *IOU*, stuck in your head for the rest of the day, I can only apologise).

Did you notice that vowel sounds are only made in the throat? They are not shaped by the lips or the tongue. Their formation is hidden away in the voice box. We can't see it. Most of us have probably never seen any voice box, let alone our own. Maybe we didn't know it is made of cartilage. Or that the sound is made by small bands of tissue contracting and expanding and altering the through movement of air.

There is sound being made. There are vowels being heard. There is a voice box.

But the thing that thinks it made that happen - this idea of me - has no idea how it happened, let alone being the one that is moving each of those bands of tissue.

What voiced those letters then?

Intelligence is making the sounds. Intelligence knows how that works and how to make it happen.

But the conscious identified mind? It doesn't know anything. It is a narrator. It is an on-going creative scenario maker. It is not the doer. It doesn't control actions, reactions, movement, responses, stasis, balance.

When we believe the idea of ourselves as 'the do-er', we are believing ourselves to be somehow separate from and controlling this Intelligence.

But what if that is not what we are at all. What if what we are really is the Intelligence that moves the air through the voice box?

In this chapter we look at what gives the illusion of a mind or a self that is separated out from Universal Intelligence.

We are considering that we are literally, *the* universal organising, all-knowing Intelligence of life itself. Not separate from it in any way. We *are* it.

This is impossible for the identified mind to grasp because its narrative is based on separation. And separation is based on the belief in control and free will.

'I am a separate entity. I make decisions. I am in control (or I should be in control) of what I do, what I think, what I believe. I made the vowel sounds. I decided to make the sound and I made them appear.'

The belief that we are a separate controlling, deciding, doing entity is absolutely fundamental to the idea of what we are.

Challenges to this belief are vehemently resisted.

It sounds sacrilegious. It sounds like our existence is being denied.

But challenge it we must.

And through that challenge our existence becomes more actual, fundamental and true than we could ever imagine.

If we eat a chocolate bar, billions of responses take place in the body to bring the body back into balance following that ingestion of milk solids, cocoa and sugar.

There is no separate 'me' in control of that.

"OK," you might say. "But the decision to eat the chocolate bar in the first place? That's me. I decided that. I'm in control of that."

Similarly, we could say 'I decided to say those vowel sounds.'

For the chocolate, where did that decision emerge from? What calculations were being made in the body - hunger, taste preference, desire? How did the impulse 'eat chocolate' arrive in the subconscious and then conscious mind? What decides which thoughts are believable? What learned the concept of chocolate in the first place?

And for saying the vowels, what decided whether it made sense to say them or not? Were they said? If so where did that reality of openness and acceptance of the invitation come from? Were they not said? What decided that it would be better to simply continue reading? What created those inner worlds of agreement or disagreement?

There are two areas that are particularly relevant when it comes to the Intelligence of being and these are: control and free will.

Free will is the belief that I am a separate individual and I am making choices that are objective, that are uninfluenced, that are the result of analysis and decision making by an independent deciding me.

Free will would mean that the 'I' I think I am has the ability to separate itself out from all learned influence, from all learned beliefs, all learned ideas, all learned conditioning and make an independent, objective decision.

It would mean that the mind is a separate independent deciding mind. I am an independent force of choosing and decision-making. This belief is fundamental to the idea of ourselves as separate from the whole.

David Bohm, the theoretical physicist, said: *"We have to believe in free will, we have no choice"*. We *do* have to believe in freewill because it is essential to the concept of a separate self. And we have no choice because all beliefs are simply what are absorbed by the system. There is no chooser of beliefs. There is just believing.

This belief that I am the decider, I am the doer, I am the objective independent decision maker is at the heart of ourselves as separate from the Intelligence of life. But even if we were to spend just a couple of minutes hanging out in the idea of free will, it becomes obvious there is just no basis for it.

At the same time, let's be clear that we are not saying there are no choices. Choices are being made all the time. Every word, every gesture, every movement, every preference (from tea or coffee, sit down, stand up, from the tiniest "when will I blink?" to "which country shall I invade next?")... there are billions of choices constantly being made.

But there is no separate decider choosing. Choices are being made by the programming of the system. They are the result of infinite layers of learning which were simply acquired because the system was wired to learn. Behaviour is impersonal.

There is no possibility that a decision could have been made another way. There is no possibility of separating out any decision from the history and pre-history that led to it.

Everything is building on and reacting to what has come before, what has been learned, what has been absorbed as the way to be, the way to behave, what has been wired into the body-mind system. Information learned and handed down through millennia down to this articulation right now.

Billions of choices. No free will. No free will because there is no individual decider.

Yet the identified mind hangs out in the beliefs that there is a me that is choosing or should choose. It looks like I am responsible for what has been learned and done.

Exploring the non-existence of free will can be enormously confronting because when the mind is identified with itself as the doer, as the controller, the chooser, the belief in free will is critical.

It looks as though we are taking away the central core of the self and, for a mind that has spent a life-time trying to stabilise that self, this is terrifying. It is as though an earthquake is rumbling beneath the precarious constructions of self belief that we are so desperate to reinforce.

It might be that the mind is in survival mode now. It must go into survival mode when the construction of separation is shaken. Because if it doesn't have that self belief, it has nothing.

Because of that belief in free will, blame and self blame are the foundations of experience. If there's no self that has free will, then shame and guilt have no founding whatsoever.

Yet, when we wake up at 0300 in the morning feeling so shameful, it is because identification is in overdrive. It is because the belief in free will is absolute.

It might be hard to hear. But hang out in it. Ask yourself, how does the hand move? How does the eye move? How does breathing happen? How does speech happen? How does listening happen?

The mind doesn't know these things, yet they are all happening. The identified mind believing that it is the doer is itself the veil.

What we are, this Universal Intelligence, is present everywhere. Always. All time. In deepest sleep, in the most concentrated analytical focus, in deepest relaxation, in laughter, in playfulness. Intelligence is organising it all. It is what we are. And an identified mind, believing itself to be separate, cannot fathom it.

This leads us on to the idea of control. Because when there is a belief in free will, there will inevitably be the need for control and the idea that 'I' should be in control of everything.

This attempt to control - emotions, experience, thoughts, beliefs - is the source of all our suffering. The belief in free will gives rise to the idea "I should be in control here. I should be able to control this, because I'm an independent agent. I'm in charge of the body. I'm in charge of thoughts. I'm in charge of beliefs. I'm in charge of emotions. I *should* be able to stop everything that I don't want and make everything that I want to happen".

And 'I' can't. Because that 'I' in that moment is a belief in myself as separate from Universal Intelligence. It is a belief in an entity that does not exist. An entity that is only a product of conditioned belief.

There is the belief in free-will, the belief in ourselves as the do-er, the desire for control and now there is resentment and resistance and the fight with reality, because "This should be different. This doesn't match up with my idea of how things should be."

That is because I believe I should be able to control everything about this body-mind that is me by association, and everything about the world out there. And I need to control the world out there so that I can be OK. I need to control this so that I can be OK.

Life then, becomes an ongoing fight for control and it sets the belief structure continually at odds with what is. It is exhausting. It takes so much effort and creates so much tension. It is absolutely futile. Not least because it revolves around an idea of me that is a total illusion.

If we go into the depth of our suffering - it becomes clear that at its heart is the desire for control and, when control is not possible, helplessness and victim-identification set in. It is vigilance or despair - no middle ground.

This comes from the belief that I am separate from Universal Intelligence. In fact it pits me, the entity, *against* Universal Intelligence.

The belief says: "I am separate from that Intelligence that is bringing the perfect amount of sunlight, oxygen, nourishment, water and nutrients. I am separate from the Intelligence that is running the body. I am separate from all of that and I have to run this show here. It is all on my shoulders".

There is no one choosing this belief. When the conditioning of separation took place within a precarious environment, control looked necessary. The idea of control, and the idea of blame and self-blame, are embedded into the identity and built on over the years. It looks like my survival is there. To loosen that grip of control might look too dangerous. "If I let go of these reins for one second, I'm going to die. What will become of me? What will become of my family, my children, my job, my well-being? I have to have this firm grip."

But the idea of ourselves as the conscious doer, the decider, the chooser can never be separate from the whole. It is the *product* of the Intelligence. It is not the originator of it. Intelligence is creating an idea of mind. It is running the body. It is firing neurons and powering a subconscious storehouse of data. The idea of myself as somehow separate from that and yet in charge of it all has no logic to it.

This takes the weight off the shoulders of a non-existent self ☺. There is no job for the self to do. It believes there is. When it believes it has to control and dictate, when it has to defend and protect and maintain and be vigilant, there is so much for it to do. Life becomes an on-going effort of exhaustion and stress. The mind is in overload. The brain is in overload. The body is in tension. But there is no job for the mind to do. It does not have to run the show. It is not responsible for survival.

The whole body can relax in that space. The mind can settle and soften. An experience of what we are, aligned to the truth of infinite and absolute Intelligence is the space in which dysfunctional conditioning dissolves away.

There is only Intelligence.

And everything - vowel sounds, voice boxes, chocolate and 1980s bands included - begins there.

HOW INTELLIGENCE IS REVEALED

Once you begin to realise that you yourself are divine just by the fact that you have a mind and a universal intelligence that backs up your form, you are already zooming ahead. The rest will happen almost automatically.
Wayne W. Dyer

Between our house and our neighbour's, is a fence about eight feet tall. I watched my cat, Lottie, at the base of the fence, looking up at the top edge. Her body was poised ready to leap. The calculations that were going on in her brain and body were visible. Tiny shifts of muscles. Micro-shuffling of paws. Eyes intently focused, head tilting slightly from side to side, up and down, gauging distance.

She leapt. Front paws, then back paws landing on the top of a 5 cm wide fence, eight times her height. The body absorbing the momentum of the jump so that she remained on the top.

Tail moving as a counter balance. A perfect leap. (She's a cat, and a Norwegian Forest at that, it's her thing.)

Intelligence in action. Data and information in form. There is a simplicity in the enormous complexity of life taking form. There is absolute straight-forwardness in the infinite bytes of data available.

How does the human mind and experience of being settle back into this infinite simplicity and straight-forwardness? How does the miracle of Intelligence that we really are become the lived experience?

One way is through the exploration of what the mind really is.

Exploring, not from an attempt to fix the mind, or control the experiences or manage emotions - as that plays straight into the idea that the Intelligence we are is separate from the whole.

But from genuine curiosity.

This is where psychology can come into its own. This has to be its future.

Because the deeper the investigation into the mind, its patterns, beliefs and tendencies, the clearer it becomes that there is no separate, individual self making any of that happen. The concept of the self is not the controller of these patterns, beliefs and tendencies. It is not the originator of them. *It is the product of them.*

This is fascinating and it is a liberation. It is the ending of the loop of personal identification.

Many of us are driven to seeking answers, from the knowing that there is something more, something missing in the way the self and life appear. And the chances are that this seeking was confused. It was always an attempt to fix the 'do-er', to find a way to control experience so that the separation could be stabilised.

The seeking might have taken us through so many different therapies and interventions. And none of it could work because at its core was the belief that 'this will fix in place this separate me' or this will bring about control over this emotion or that belief or that experience. It was circling around an illusion.

Now, though all psychological techniques, can be understood differently. They are a way of understanding and intervening with a psychological system that isn't being orchestrated by an individual, controlling self. All behaviours and perceptions are the result of learned conditioning *and there was no separate learner*.

The first invitation of this section, therefore, is to pick up books or videos about the mind and behaviour that do not stop at the idea of an individual controlling, deciding self and which instead question what that self really is.

In other words, to go so deeply into what the self is that it dissolves before our eyes.

Then we can start to look at the world of apparent form. The enormity of this conversation is that it allows for a greater and more open exploration of the world and of reality.

When seen through the lens of the self identity, reality is distorted by the personal delusion. Perception is dictated by what has shaped the evolution of that perception. According to what has been learned, reality will appear a certain way.

Fear, need and insecurity are at the heart of the conditioned idea of separation.

We might do everything we can to avoid these feelings but, actually, in the exploration of truth, they are the gateway to freedom.

In those moments when it looks as though we are under threat and the body is going into fight or flight, we can ask ourselves 'Is there actual physical danger right now? Right now this minute?'

The answer is always 'no' because if there really was physical danger the system would be dealing with it. The Intelligence would be running the show, moving the body, responding, preserving life in this form. In the same way that Lottie runs from the sound of a car engine starting up or a dog barking.

What is really at stake in our everyday fear and insecurity is not the physical body, it is this idea of ourselves as the controller, that has to survive. What is at stake is the thing that gets scared when things aren't known, or that feels it has to nail everything down, control everything, predict everything, know what's going to happen. This is the insanity of all of us. The mind's fears of its own projections.

And, as that falls away, a sensory playground appears with everything to explore. As the limitations, fears, shames and insecurities of the identity fall away the body-mind is liberated to immerse itself in its relationships and surroundings in a way that might not ever have been possible.

There is marvel at the Intelligence of life that we are and what that Intelligence creates.

Intelligence is playing in the world of form, responding to it, learning, understanding.

It is that simple. And that can become the blueprint for the rest of our lives. This is complete alignment to truth. It is the body-mind system freed up to deal only with reality, no longer at war with its own confusion. Intelligence responding to now, to what is true.

This is a system, now deeply relaxed and aligned, simply responding to reality.

This is liberation and intimacy.

And in that liberation, we realise this body-mind does the human / non-Norwegian cat equivalent of scaling eight foot fences all day every day.

Effortless.

Natural.

Miraculous.

Intelligence in action.

IN SUMMARY...

Intelligence...

WHAT IS IT?

The universal, organising force.

The precursor, pre-requisite and enabler of all intellectual phenomena.

What veils it?

The belief that I am an independent chooser that is somehow separate from this intelligence.

The unquestioned conviction in free will.

The on-going attempt to secure the idea of ourselves through control, seeking and resistance.

What reveals it?

Curiosity about all behaviour, words and decision making - where is that coming from?

'No-self accountability' - the recognition that words and behaviours are being generated by this body-mind system even if there is no self controlling them.

PART IV
ALIVENESS

Being is totally whole just being. And it is alive and fleshy and sexy and juicy and immediately this; it's not some concept about 'there's no-one here'. It's not some concept about 'there's nowhere to go'. It's the aliveness that's in that body right now. There is pure beingness, pure aliveness.
Tony Parsons

Once upon a time, in ancient Greece, the Emperor was dying and it was time for his first born, Prince Ochiego to take over his father's role.

In preparation for the event, the most famous portrait artist in the Empire was brought to the Palace. The new Emperor's portrait would be worked into the mosaic Palace walls alongside the portraits of all his fore-fathers.

Prince Ochiego sat for many sittings. The artist brought all of his talent, experience and ability to creating what he knew would be a masterpiece.

Eventually the Emperor breathed his last breath and immediately the ceremony was arranged to announce the accession.

All of the Empire's most illustrious leaders were gathered into the Palace and when the portrait was unveiled at the end of ceremony, the whole room gasped.

It was an incredible feat of artistry and brilliance.

Every detail was luminous. The many shades and shadows of his skin. The lustre in his eyes. The gentle curl of his eyelashes and sweep of his brow. The vitality of the limbs. It seemed more alive than life itself.

The new Emperor was tremendously proud of the portrait. He took every opportunity he could find to walk past it. He looked at the genius of the art work, the beauty of the image and it made him believe he *was* someone. Even just a five minute glance was enough to boost him for the rest of the day.

He gave the portrait an affectionate moniker, 'Ego', a shortened form of his own name. He insisted that anyone visiting the Palace should leave a gift at the feet of Ego. He decreed that the portrait must be cleaned every day with water from the spring. He had the windows of the Great Hall moved so that the light would only shine on it from certain directions. He insisted that the portrait receive attention at all times and a rota was drawn up for Palace officials to take turns in admiring the perfection.

Then one day the Emperor was walking in the gardens when he felt a terrible tremble move through the ground beneath his feet. An earthquake was ravaging the land and the Palace walls were shaking.

He could think of only one thing.

"The portrait," he shouted, running towards the Palace. "Ego. Save Ego. Save the portrait"

But it was too late. The portrait was crumbling along with everything else.

This was the worst happening imaginable.

What would he be without it?

He flung himself on the floor in despair. He was nothing now. He sobbed, prepared to never see the world again.

For hours he lay there. Distraught. No one could comfort him. It was over. His life was finished.

He lay there. And, after a while, he noticed he was uncomfortable.

He moved his legs.

Then his arms.

Eventually, he propped himself up and stretched his back.

He started to feel a little hungry and anyway he needed to use the Royal Bathroom.

He looked around at the rubble.

It slowly came to him that there were people to help, a Palace to rebuild, and a portrait to… well… for some reason, that didn't seem so interesting any more.

So he stood up, brushed the dust off his robe and got on with what he was there to do.

WE ARE ALIVENESS

It's not the meaning of life we seek but our aliveness. Once we have that, the meaning of life is obvious.
Anodea Judith

My father was very ill with leukaemia. His death was expected and my Mum was with him. She said afterwards, "It was as though from one moment to the next he was there and not there.'

The body, of course, was identical from one moment to the next. Nothing had changed really. And yet, the movement of life out of that form was completely obvious. *He* was no longer there. My father was not the body, which was still there on the bed. He was the life that had moved out of that body.

Life, Aliveness, life-force, energy...

What makes this so remarkable and astonishing, is that when we think of what we are, we completely disregard 'life', don't we?

We think that we are a doer, a decider. We think we are the content of beliefs and experience. We think we are the adjectives and the labels that we have acquired over the years. We think we are the body, the mind, the thoughts. We think that we are everything we identity with - jobs, relationships, earnings, roles, health...

But what would any of this be without life that is animating this form? Without life, *I* would not exist in the form that I exist currently. Every single aspect of this form, of all of these beliefs, of all of these thoughts, of all of this experience of the appearance of all other people, all other situations and circumstances, all of it is one hundred percent dependent on the Aliveness that brings it into existence, that animates it.

It is startling how the mind, how the identity, the self idea, believes it is something real and that it is something that exists independently of life, that somehow the identity itself really is the life giver.

All we are, can be is Aliveness. And life cannot be known or understood. It is prior to understanding. Prior to mind. Prior to brain.

It cannot be isolated out of the form, the cell, the plant or the animal because without the form, even though it is all there is, it is not observable in any way.

It is only in the form that the life-force, this invisible, infinite, absolute can be perceived. It can't be described in any way. There is no relativity to it. No comparison. It is life. Infinite and absolute.

Aliveness defies conceptualisation and tangibility. Yet it is known. It is known that that is what we are.

What is life?

Impossible to say, isn't it? All we have as reference is the form - the quantum physics of atomic particles, the biology of fertilisation, the chemistry of photosynthesis, the neurology of synapses firing...

We can't reach an understanding of life without the form.

All we know is that when it leaves the form, that form in that particular expression is no more. The life-force moves out of the human form and then in come billions of other forms, all equally animated by this same life-force, powered by this same life-force that will decompose the body, but the life that was powering the human form in total is no longer there.

One moment we are there, animated form and then the next moment, *we are* gone but only because the life we really are has moved out.

That means that we must be the animating force. We are this energetic, indefinable, absolute, infinite... what word do we use..? Force...? Power...? Energy...? It defies all description.

It cannot be described but there is so much that can fall away. If what we are is Aliveness, then any belief in separation and difference must go, any belief in transience and objectivity.

Speaking, listening, laughing, moving, thinking, believing - all of it only possible because of this animating force. What are we - the temporary, momentary form? The fleeting activity? Or the life that brings that form and activity into existence.

The form is not us. The activity is not us. We are the animating force bringing it to life.

And doing it perfectly.

HOW ALIVENESS IS VEILED

The only two things in our lives are aliveness and patterns that block our aliveness.
Werner Erhard

I was a fairly junior PR consultant in an agency in London and my boss asked me to run a brainstorming session with a client who was known to be quite difficult. I spent ages preparing for this session with prompts and suggestions to get ideas flowing.

It got off to a bad start and went downhill as it became clear he wasn't expecting a brainstorming session at all. He wanted to be presented with ideas that he could then choose from. Thirty minutes in, he stands up, slams his hands on the table, strides to the door, flings it open and shouts down *the entire length of the office* to my boss at the far end 'FIONA! THIS IS THE WORST MEETING I HAVE EVER BEEN IN. GET CLARE DIMOND OFF THIS ACCOUNT'.

What a nasty thing to do, right? And what I am about to say doesn't excuse his behaviour - keep that in mind.

This felt like the end of the world for me. Not only was I humiliated in front of all my colleagues in the meeting and my boss (who I loved and deeply respected. Shout out to you, Fiona!), I had been shamed in front of the whole office. It felt like death. I ran into the toilets crying and I couldn't leave until everyone had gone home for the day.

That evening, I was going away for the weekend with my boyfriend and his family to a stunning place on the coast. I couldn't stop crying to look at the view. His brother announced his engagement to his lovely girlfriend. I could barely stop crying enough to congratulate them.

I was dying.

I was dying.

What was that *I*?

It was the *I* of self-esteem, the social me, the *I* of other people's opinion and regard, it was the image of me. It absolutely felt like death because everything I thought I was and believed I had to protect looked like it was being destroyed.

And yet nothing had changed in the Aliveness animating the body. Indeed that feeling of death— which was the experience of humiliation, shame, isolation, exposure, failure—was only possible *because* of the Aliveness.

In other words, Aliveness was making possible the experience of death. How's that for irony?

And this is why the Aliveness we are is continually veiled. Because it looks like our survival is under threat.

This is truly the invisible elephant in the room.

Incredible that it's overlooked, but it happens all the time doesn't it?

The human mind is wired for social integration. It is wired for interaction. It is wired to believe and conceptualise. It is wired for intrigue and comparison. It is wired to create identity. It is wired for the taking literally of appearance. It is wired to protect its idea of itself.

There are many reasons for this wiring. The survival of the human form, particularly as a baby and child, but also through to old age, depends on other people. It is to the advantage of the 'body-mind' to engage with the world of form, to interact, to get involved with the details, the intricacies. It is an advantage for the brain to be wired for social engagement, for involvement with others. It is an advantage to have a superpower mind that can imagine, create, predict, conceptualise, categorise…

This is an advantage.

But when this mind and its creations are taken as unquestioned reality, as *what we are*, it can lead to an impossible fight for survival.

When the mind is immersed in the fight and flight that comes from a believed idea of what we are and of what the world is, it looks so real that this is the lived experience of truth. It is all-encompassing because it looks as if our survival is at stake. It looks like *the life we are* is under threat.

Except in those moments, attention is not focused on life. It is focused on the representative of life, the concept of self, the identity, the beliefs of what we are, the opinions of others. Life is not under threat. The life we are is untouched. And yet certain situations, relationships or brainstorms-that-shouldn't-have-been-a-brainstorm look like life and death.

The mind is immersed in the story, having no idea that it is generating those stories itself. It is looking in the stories for its safety and survival. The more it does that, the more lost it becomes and the more the infinite and absolute life we are is over-looked.

It is the ultimate irony that in this life and death struggle, this fight for survival, the life force that is the only truth, which is completely untouched and which isn't going anywhere, isn't even noticed.

It's like being in the cinema watching the most engrossing film imaginable. The acting, the script, the cinematography is so flawless that there's not a single second's thought that this isn't real.

In that immersion, we are on the edge of our seats, feeling the passions of the characters, swept away. Not for one moment in that lostness is there a thought of the cinema, the seat, the projection, other people in the room, of the director, the production house, the actors, the make up, the costumes... nothing. We are utterly consumed by the content.

And then the film is over and we emerge from the cinema, with beliefs, understanding, reality changed in some way by what we have just witnessed. As Robert McKee, the scriptwriting genius, says, "Story isn't a flight from reality but a vehicle that carries us on our search for reality, our best effort to make sense out of the anarchy of existence."

The point, in that moment, in the cinema, *is* to be lost in the content.

Could that be the point of life in form?

To have these moments, these experiences of ourselves as something that we're not? And through these experiences to realise something true and permanent?

The only way to experience the Aliveness that we are— infinite, absolute, all powerful, everywhere, every thing— is to experience ourselves as something other than that.

Could it be that the temporary experience of ourselves as limited, or isolated and then the subsequent knowing of ourselves as beyond limit is the point of life in this form?

This would be the perfection of the design. The eventual understanding of ourselves as the animating force *and* its engagement or localisation in this world of temporary form.

Both are available.

But, while the mind is fully identified and while survival depends on the protection of that identity, then any sense of ourselves as being life itself is completely lost.

The survival of the concept of being hides the enormity of what we are. It shrinks us to this tiny meaningful fight for survival.

It brings all attention to that fragile me and, in the process, coastal views and engagements of loved ones are completely missed.

A fight for survival, in other words, that has absolutely nothing to do with life.

HOW ALIVENESS IS REVEALED

Spiritual awakening is becoming awake to the aliveness of this moment.
Eckhart Tolle

It is fascinating how in that moment of public embarrassment, the only thing that mattered was ME. Crying in the toilets - me. Crying in the car - me. Beautiful holiday location - me. Major, wonderful life announcement from beloved friends - me. That momentary death brought all focus, all attention, all resources onto the thing that looked to be under threat - me.

I might cringe at it now, 30 years on, but it will continue to happen every time survival (in other words the identity) looks to be under threat. The suffering of apparent rejection, indifference, exclusion, shame, fear and insecurity will continue to drive the lived experience of being alive into survival mode.

It's no wonder that nature, the sea, the sky, our pets and plants rarely challenge our sense of survival in the way other people do. Other people press the buttons and flick the triggers of all our inner-most vulnerabilities and insecurities.

And yet in all that struggle, there is nothing that has to be done to make the Aliveness more present in the body. The Aliveness is everything already. 'What I am' is not more alive if the mind is aligned to that Aliveness or whether it is lost in its own imagined demise.

Nevertheless, the alignment of our experience to the true nature of infinite and absolute Aliveness brings the body-mind system back to reality. It is restful. It is sane. The body is designed to respond to information that is happening right now.

How does this happen? How does the vigilance of survival end? What brings the fight against the mind's own projections to a close?

This is where suffering plays a tremendously powerful role.

Suffering can take us deeper into the life-and-death tension, deeper into the film (as it did for me after that meeting).

Or it is a signal to the system that the mind is momentarily lost in a fight for survival within its own concepts.

When we are confronted or offended or rejected by someone, we might have that contraction of defence, that immediate sense of separation.

That feeling of contraction is a gift.

It is information.

It is a signal to be still.

A moment of pause to see what that 'me' really is.

IN SUMMARY...

Aliveness...

WHAT IS IT?

The pre-requisite to everything. Without aliveness, nothing.

The force animating the body and all perception.

What veils it?

The fight for the survival of an idea of ourselves that is separate from aliveness.

The life and death drama of everyday life that has nothing to do with physical survival.

What reveals it?

Suffering and the tension of threat to the identity being understood.

Curiosity about what seems to be at stake in moments of fear, shame and insecurity.

PART V
WHOLENESS

※

In other words, in reality, there are not two things—one, the screen and two, the document or image. There is just the screen. Two things (or a multiplicity and diversity of things) only come into apparent existence when their true reality—the screen—is overlooked.

Rupert Spira

Once upon a time, a wave rose up from the ocean. It felt alone and a bit lost. It felt disconnected somehow. Not really safe. Like it didn't fit in. Something was missing.

It wondered how it could feel less insecure.

'I know', thought the wave. 'It's because no one is noticing me. Perhaps if I had more attention. Perhaps if all the other waves noticed and respected me then I would feel more secure.'

The wave tried to make itself different from the other waves. It made itself bigger, then smaller, frothier then calmer but it didn't work. It still felt out of sorts.

'Maybe I need to be more like all the other waves', it thought. 'Maybe that's why I feel a bit lonely and isolated. I need to be more similar.'

And so the wave copied the movements, the rise and fall and the sounds of the other waves but it didn't feel any better.

'Maybe if I was more beautiful…"

So the wave twisted and turned to catch the rays of the evening sunset. It glowed purple and orange. It received a lot of admiration but it still felt like something wasn't right.

A bigger wave moved alongside. 'What's up with you?', it asked.

'I don't feel right' said the first wave. 'I feel separate. Like I don't belong. Can you help?'

'Yes of course. Watch me carefully.'

And the bigger wave slowly, easily, effortlessly sank back into the ocean before appearing again.

'Well…?' said the first wave.

'Well what?' said the second wave.

'I'm waiting for you to tell me. How do I stop feeling so alone?'

'Watch me again,' said the second wave and it sank back into the ocean. Disappearing completely and then re-emerging.

'I still don't get it. Please just tell me.' said the first wave. 'How do I stop feeling so alone…?'

And again, the bigger wave sank back into the ocean.

It took the rest of the day of this being repeated until the little wave suddenly realised.

'Ahhhh…' it said and laughed. 'I get it! Sorry it took me so long.'

The big wave smiled. 'That's OK.'

Time wasn't an issue.

There was nowhere else that either of them had to be.

There was nowhere else that either of them *could* be.

WE ARE WHOLE

'Non-duality' is... a word that points to an intimacy, a love beyond words, right at the heart of present moment experience. It's a word that points us back Home. And despite the compelling appearance of separation and diversity there is only one universal essence, one reality. Oneness is all there is – and we are included.

Jeff Foster

Let's close our eyes and think of a tree. And let's make it a specific tree we are thinking of. A tree from our past perhaps. Or maybe a tree near where we are living now.

Is the tree we are thinking of real? The obvious answer is 'Yes. Of course it is. It is a real tree I'm thinking of'.

But the tree in our minds isn't real, is it?

There is no actual tree there. A collection of neurones creating an idea of a tree but no actual tree.

The tree exists in mind, and mind doesn't really exist anywhere because the moment we move on and we talk about tables or candles or fire... where's 'tree' gone? It doesn't exist any more, it has gone.

'Well OK you might say but come with me.' And we'd go together until we were standing right outside the tree you'd been thinking of and you might say,

'Fair enough, Clare. The tree I was thinking of was just in my mind. But this tree now is real and separate and objectively as it appears to be.'

And that is very hard to argue with.

That seems like an incontrovertible argument against Wholeness. The world is divided into separate parts, separate objects all of which look absolutely real and separate.

You might now say 'Stop with all the Wholeness, spiritual, non-dual, advaita nonsense, Clare. There are obviously separate things. There is a real tree here. It is separate from us. It is separate from other trees. Separation is reality and Wholeness is a woo-woo myth.'

A tree is a tree, after all!

But let's pause here for a moment.

Let's pause because that unquestioned assumption of separation and objectivity is the source of all our suffering.

We could begin by asking ourselves how does that tree come into our experience?

It can only be through perception. Everything about the tree is a wealth of sensory information at conscious and subconscious levels. This information forms the impression of a tree in the mind.

And this impression is unique to that sensory collection of data and that interpreting mind.

Because what is a tree to a fly on a leaf?

What is a tree to an earth worm in the soil, to a bird, to a fungus, to me, to you…?

The tree I experience is a unique, temporary construct.

Embedded into my perception are all of the associations, the memories, the meaning, the language, the definitions. All of that is a mental structure of agreement, none of which has any concrete reality to it. It is hard for the mind to see this because what is perceived within that conscious space looks like concrete reality.

We think we see an objective tree, absolutely real, but everything about that perception is filtered and distorted according to perceptual limits and to what is known and believed. And that perception is possible because of Consciousness, Aliveness. The infinite and absolute brings it into existence. The subjective only exists because of what is beyond subjectivity, the absolute.

At that level, that experiential level, we can consider that there literally is no separate other. There actually is no thing. Non dual. There are not two things. There is just an experience, a sensory experience of energetic data interpreted by mind. And that experience doesn't really exist anywhere - certainly not 'out there'.

And then you might go over to the tree with some serious looking piece of equipment, saw off a branch, come back over to where I am standing and hit me on the arm with it. Possibly with slightly more force than was strictly warranted.

'Now tell me that isn't real Clare' you might say.

And now there might be pain, a bruise (blood even if the branch is particularly spiky).

And all of that looks objectively real. Yet it is no different. Everything about the experience remains a subjective appearance of separation brought into existence by the inseparable.

And this is the paradox. It doesn't mean there isn't a tree, or a branch, or a wallop on the arm, or a me or a you. It just means that *how* all of that appears is a momentary creation of perception and that the perception belongs to the perceiver, not to the tree, branch, pain or bruise. In other words the experience cannot be separate from the perceiver. It *is* the perceiver.

And what enables that idea of separation to exist? It is the absolute and infinite. It is Consciousness, Aliveness, Intelligence - indivisible, unlocatable, timeless, no beginning, no end.

Without this, no experience of ourselves, no experience of a world, no experience of separation.

We can only talk about 'Wholeness' as a concept and of course that creates immediate division. But nevertheless it points the attention in the direction of what is intangible, non-material, the neither objective nor subjective, beyond mind, beyond perception, beyond relativity.

This is the profoundly spiritual, deeply majestic essence that is indicated in non-dual teachings. Whenever there's a mention of Wholeness or Oneness, it is this. And, however we define it, it doesn't matter. The words that we put on it, they will never be right, they will never be able to convey what lies behind the words, behind the mind, behind experience, behind any belief or idea of what we are.

It is simply the impossibility of there actually being a fixed, objective, separate me and other, no matter what it looks like in our daily life. And it is the pointing to the indivisible, indefinable existence that is prior to the mind's creation of separation.

This is not the end of existence or presence. We *know* we exist. Existence does not change through this exploration, other than to become more and more obviously the truth of what we are.

The I of existence, of presence does not change with belief, thought, emotion because it is prior to all of that. It allows all of that. The Wholeness of existence is the only thing that can be truthfully known.

And now I'm going to move this branch before anyone gets hurt.

HOW WHOLENESS IS VEILED

Most of us are dragged towards wholeness.
Marion Woodman

There is a video from a chimpanzee sanctuary of chimps who had been held for over 30 years in captivity for medical research being released into nature for the first time. It is impossible to watch the scenes of them hugging each other, dancing and exploring without being deeply moved.

A mind trapped in a lifetime of fighting its own limited view of itself and then released into sanity, reality, presence is our mental equivalent of this freedom. It is right and true. It resonates deep with our essential being, we know it is our nature. To know freedom and alignment through their opposites is to have the most profound experience of truth.

There is an adage in yoga that the pose we find most awkward and inaccessible in our first class will ultimately become our favourite pose.

We see this elsewhere.

The people we clash with on first meeting can become the people we love and admire the most. The tasks we avoid at all cost can become the areas where we find the greatest freedom. The aspects of our lives and personalities that we are ashamed of or try to hide or deny can become our life's celebration. The things we find most difficult and confronting can become a surprising source of fascination and pleasure.

These areas of life where we feel lacking, incapable or threatened are always the areas to see what is there to be seen, feel what is there to be felt, allow to fall away what is there to fall away.

These are our greatest gifts. It is these areas in which the lived experience of separation, the on-going belief in the object is as far as possible from what is really true. It is where the resistance, whether physical, mental or emotional is indicating a depth of freedom to be discovered.

It's almost impossible to imagine in that moment of incompleteness though, isn't it? In the moment of comparison, or self-hate or anger or shame, or limitation all we want to do is escape, run, hide, give up.

On-going unconscious reaction, on-going battles to secure the self, on-going fights with a reality that is only ever a projection of our inner-most shame, insecurity and fears is absolutely exhausting. It takes all the energy, attention and resources.

The essential Wholeness of our being is veiled by the vicious circle of a mind trying to find its way back to that completeness. It is in the knowing of our true nature that the mind can operate so powerfully, so cleanly, so in tune, so sanely.

Yet it is trying to find "Home", trying to find its way back through an unquestioned belief in a separate self and separate world.

It is trying to control the world and itself, not realising that these are concepts. The more desperate it is to find its way Home, the more it struggles against itself. And the more it struggles against itself, the more desperate it is to find Home. And on it goes. It is a vicious circle.

In other words, the areas that represent the most threat to our idea of ourselves take all the focus and look the most hopeless. Of course they do. These are the areas where we look most separate, most isolated, most lacking, with most to defend. They are gripping and life-and-death important.

But through curiosity, this un-winnable, futile, debilitating battle ceases. And now, just as when, in yoga, we constrict then release a part of the body, that released area of our life is filled with fresh energy, fresh oxygen, fresh potential. There is a vitality which might not have been experienced since childhood.

And all of this is not in spite of, but *because of* the restriction, the veils. The difficulty itself is the gateway to a greater understanding and capacity, to a different, clearer, more open version of self and reality.

Life continually provides these areas of discovery because they are a direct manifestation of the inside conditioning of lack appearing outside and therefore these areas are the space in which healing takes place.

The chimps, held captive, were dependent on humans for release.

What is the mind, held captive, dependent on?

Nothing.

And we've got a lifetime to discover it.

HOW WHOLENESS IS REVEALED

*The purpose of our journey is to
restore ourselves to wholeness*
Debbie Ford

For Byron Katie, it was waking up on the floor of her residential care home watching a cockroach crawl over her foot.

For Eckhart Tolle, it was what he described as 'an inner transformation' after decades of depression.

For Jeff Foster, it was the point of absolute despair 'transform or commit suicide. There was no other option.'

For Roger Linden, it was on a walk through Hamstead Heath in London 'one second it was Roger - me - walking along the path, and the next moment it was as if something dissolved. And it took a fraction of a second and it was realised, 'Oh there is no separate me'.

For Rupert Spira, it was at a young age through deep resonance with non-dual teachings.

For Tony Parsons, there had been the sense even as young as seven years old that 'everything that was happening was somehow saying something other than me being separate.'

For Syd Banks, it was a conversation with a psychologist and the words, 'You just think you're insecure'.

And so many other examples (many of which are beautifully told in the book 'Conversations in non-duality, twenty six awakenings' edited by Eleonora Gilbert.)

There is clearly no set way that Wholeness is revealed.

Many teachers describe reaching absolute rock bottom, suicidal, hopeless, despairing and, in that moment of everything being stripped away, there is the realisation of what remains that is entirely unaffected.

But this does not have to happen. Many other teachers describe sudden realisations while out in nature or in the city, a sentence or a few words in a talk given by a teacher that profoundly shake the foundations of believed separation.

For others it is an on-going dissolution of what is not true. A deeper reality being revealed in each interaction in which the sense of self appears under threat.

There is no prescription other than it has to involve the falling away of what was once believed, the structure of belief that says I am this and the world is that.

In this chapter we are exploring what allows the mind to settle back into that truth. Many would say it doesn't have to. It doesn't need to, because the mind doesn't really exist, it is simply momentary, transient experience. And on that basis, it could be said that it is irrelevant.

This is a tough one. It's something that I find intriguing in this teaching. It is a very, very valid proposition. If life *is* just this moment right now and this moment only consists of the essence of being-ness, then, whatever the experience is doesn't matter because the Wholeness, the totality, the is-ness contains it all. The experience, whatever it is, is not separate from the fundamental truth.

This is the dilemma we have in this conversation.

There is no possibility that "what we are" isn't already Home. We already are the thing. Which is why many non-dual teachers are absolutely uncompromising in closing down any conversation about self or form. The only issue is the thought of individuality and that issue or thought doesn't exist.

Yet, at the same time, this experience of being other, of being isolated and separate – like a wave imagining itself separate from the ocean – that experience is torture. Because the whole system knows deep down that it is not true. To experience ourselves as being something that is separate from truth creates enormous suffering.

So what do we do? Where do we go with that? How can the wave realise it is the ocean? And yes, the moment we start thinking in terms of a wave, we're already creating an idea of separation. Talking about the mind, talking about us, me, you, talking about suffering, experience, reality… all these things are adding in more and more elements of separation. So what do we do?

It seems to me, that there is value in finding ways for the experience of what we are, for the knowing of what we are, to align with what we know is true.

I would go so far as to say that (ironically) the only purpose to our life is to realise that there is no separate life, that there is no separate individual for which any of this is happening.

'Seeking' has a bad name because more often than not the seeking is about the attempt to stabilise the identity, to be someone, to make the separation real. But actually, the impetus for the seeking, this sense that the lived experience of separation is not the truth of us, this is absolutely valid. It is just that the attempt to get rid of the suffering keeps the mind locked in its own creations.

Wholeness (truth, permanence, infinite, absolute) is revealed or unveiled by the dissolution of what is not real (mind, thoughts, beliefs, separation, apparent objectivity). We can see that the attempt to find Wholeness in the mind will always fail and will always lead to more of the very activity that is obscuring what is being searched for.

What allows what is not true to fall away?

That's the million dollar question isn't it? Because the more fragile the ego, the greater the desperation to solidify the sense of being, and the more the attempt to stabilise the fraction veils the Wholeness.

Enquiry is one way. And perhaps no one has encapsulated this more cleanly and simply than Byron Katie in her series of questions called 'The Work'. Instead of the mind lost in fighting its own concepts of blame, harm, victim and villain, enquiry turns the focus on to what is true. It is fascinating to watch this incredible teacher in action. We, the audience, can see the participant completely lost in their own story of separation. Byron Katie brings them back to enquiry with loving rigour. And then, it is almost as if we can see the mind reaching back beyond those beliefs that have dominated every waking hour to the foundation of existence. Is it true? The mind goes to its furthest origin and comes back with... no, it's not, none of it is true. None of it is real in the way it was believed to be.

And again, it is important to say that enquiry *in order* to find Peace or freedom will not reveal anything. The unquestioned agenda of the mind to control emotions and experience is at work and will only hide the Peace and freedom that is right here, right now.

The enquiry has to be genuinely open, no agenda, no attempt to control, no attempt to come up with the right answer or to impress the teacher or to say the right spiritual words. Simply an enquiry into truth.

Another way is the shifting of attention from what changes (mind, experience, labels, concepts, beliefs, separation) to what never changes, to what lies before all of the changing landscape of mind, to what gives rise to it.

As we saw in the previous chapter, what changes is enticing to a mind that is wired for story. It is so easy for the transient to grab the attention, especially when it seems to continually involve the life and death of our idea of self. It is no wonder that all attention is sucked into that tension-filled drama.

This is a shift from the drama, from the tension, from the intrigue and the survival of being this individual self in this world of separate form. A shift to the pervasive essence of what we are, that is touched in moments of flow, in moments of absolute presence or laughter or when all barriers drop, all the thoughts drop, all the concepts drop, and there is only beingness, completely whole just being.

The glimpses of this start to become the truthful navigation for life. Whereas before, the mind was the navigation - the mind with its calculations, its judgements and its predictions, its second guessing, calculating how to orientate within a thought-created world.

The whole system starts to orientate around the understanding of Wholeness. It becomes literally a 'no-brainer'. It is the deepest most essential relaxing rejuvenating, energising, sane, truthful space for the mind to hang out in.

There is no point or value in denying these experiences of separation. It is not about turning away from them, numbing or distracting from them or spiritually overwriting them. Pretending they don't exist only makes them appear more real and more permanent. This is about staying with the experiences until the essential emptiness of them is revealed.

Let's take an example. Imagine someone who you've had a difficult relationship with, and, in the past, you might have seen them as someone to blame, as someone responsible for how you are feeling, as someone who intentionally decided to do these things that upset you.

There's a you: defensive, vulnerable, upset, offended, hurt. And there's a them, who is intentionally hurting you. At that level, the experience of the other is locked in to this apparent reality of separation, and all conversations, all memories, all interactions are taking place within that. The past gets dragged up and the future projection comes in. There is an absolutely unquestioned experience of two separate objective entities. There is me and there is them.

Then, we embark on this conversation and through it several things happen. Initially we start seeing the mirror that they represent, that every experience of them is a creation of mind and that creation of mind is coming from our own insecurities, our own shame, our own vulnerabilities.

Ideas of blame fall away as we consider that there is no self, doing these things. The behaviour of the other is just learned conditioning: *our* response to the other is learned conditioning.

We start seeing these two 'robots', these two units in a sort of dance together: a dance of conditioning, a dance of programmed reaction. That interaction of the robots becomes less and less interesting because what is the truth here? What is animating these robots? How are these robots even brought into existence?

There is now less focus on the drama of separation and the separation starts to dissolve anyway, as it is not having the attention that fuels it.

There is more space, more presence, more capacity. There is more possibility to sit with this person and hear them. There is the realisation that we are them. We *are* them. And that knowing, that falling away is our orientation now. Because, until there is that experience, that knowing, we are not in reality. We are in a made-up land of others.

That can be how Wholeness is realised everywhere but it is particularly poignant with other people because that is where the veils of separation are more and more dense, where it seems there is so much to protect.

This is a whole new orientation within truth. Any sense of contraction, or tension, suffering, or isolation is an indication that the system is momentarily operating on a programme that isn't aligned into truth.

Suffering *is* the design.

It is separation itself that reveals Wholeness.

We don't have to be Eckhard Tolle or Byron Katie. We don't have to be depressed or suicidal. We don't have to have followed spiritual gurus. We don't have to do anything.

Wholeness is simply being revealed.

In every moment, the appearance of separation is showing the only truth.

Home.

IN SUMMARY...

Wholeness

WHAT IS IT?

The impossibility of perception and the perceived being separate.

The impossibility of the truth of existence being divisible, identifiable or definable.

WHAT VEILS IT?

Identification with the divided, defined and separable.

Trying to find wholeness through the unquestioned belief in a separate self and world.

. . .

What reveals it?

Enquiry into the beliefs and the sense of separation.

Attention shifting from what changes constantly to what never changes.

PART VI
PEACE

You find peace not by rearranging the circumstances of your life, but by realising who you are at the deepest level.
Eckhart Tolle

Once upon a time, there was a Queen who wanted a new painting for the Royal Chamber, a painting that she could look at from her bed, before she went to sleep. It had to be very special, very calming. She sent messages across the kingdom announcing a competition. Whichever artist could create the most accurate representation of peace would receive a thousand gold coins.

The paintings started arriving from all over the land from all the most celebrated artists, scenes of silent mountains and valleys, tranquil forests, clear blue skies reflected in motionless lakes, misty temples, sleeping babies and animals, meditating monks. The Queen was struck by the talent, the techniques and the beauty of the pictures but there was still something missing for her. She found herself unable to choose.

The day of the announcement came. The Queen looked again at the ones she liked the most but still she felt none of them were quite what she was looking for. It was too late to cancel the event. The crowds were lining the street. She would just have to announce a winner even though, in her secret opinion, none of the paintings really represented peace.

As she passed by in her carriage on the short trip to the podium, something caught her eye. She turned to look and saw a young man holding up a blank canvas. The man was tilting and moving the canvas so that the shadows of the crowd appeared on it and then disappeared.

The Queen stopped the carriage and watched. The young man moved to stand behind a parent who was shouting at his son, the shadows of their gesticulations showing up clearly on the white square. The man moved again to stand behind a couple holding hands. The Queen could see the shadow of their arms and the tilt of their heads on the canvas. The canvas was moved to show the shape of a man sitting slumped, drunk and alone. And then moved again to show two pigeons fighting overhead on a branch.

The Queen got out of the carriage. The young man moved forward and stood so that the Queen was directly between him and the sun. She saw the shadow of her robes and crown appear inside the frame. She raised her arms . Her shadow raised its arms. She danced. Her shadow danced. She shook her fists. Her shadow shook its fists. The man tilted the canvas away from her and her shadow disappeared. All that could be seen was the blank empty space, unchanged by everything that had appeared on it. He held the canvas out, offering it to her.

The Queen took the blank frame. Smiling for the first time that day, she turned towards the podium.

WE ARE PEACE

Because we've been conditioned from birth to believe in the myth of an outside-in world, we assume the path back to wellbeing and joy and peace of mind must be through getting a better job or a better partner or working on becoming a better person.
Michael Neill

I had IVF treatment to have both of my children. For Finn, the youngest child, I went to a clinic in London that was known for their no holds barred, full-on approach. The hormonal injections I was asked to take were enormous, frequent and intense.

Over that period of time, my mind and emotions were all over the place. Intense paranoia, anger, deep sadness. And yet through it all there was, weirdly, absolute Peace. I didn't need to do anything about the thoughts or feelings. I didn't need to act on them. I didn't believe them. I knew without any question that it was all the result of the hormones disrupting my system. The emotional and mental turmoil, the paranoia, depression, anxiety, highs and lows were just a product of the injections. None of it was information about me or the world. The truth of me watched the intensity of experience change like weather.

What we are considering in HOME is that Peace is not the absence of unwanted experience. It is not the eternal sunshine of the spotless mind. It is not the guarantee that we will never feel angry, sad, rejected.

On the contrary, Peace is the openness to ALL of that. To every experience. Just for what it is.

The most fundamental form of existence, is Consciousness, Aliveness or Intelligence momentarily located in transient, sensory, perception-created form.

And this fundamental form will respond to whatever arises, moment by moment.

Our moments of profound realisation are when the lived experience or understanding of what we are returns to that truth.

(We could consider this to be what Mihaly Csikszentmihalyi termed 'flow', what Abraham Maslow referred to as 'Self Transcendence', or William James' 'Mystical Experience'.)

This is the movement through and beyond the personal. It is ultimate receptivity to every detail of experience, none of it resisted.

The understanding that the body-mind system will simply respond as Intelligence to whatever arises and that what we are is that Intelligence means that vigilance, control and projection are not required.

The Aliveness we are is fully responsive, it is available; meeting whatever is there in the moment; not trying to guard against future emotions that might come in; just meeting what is there because that is reality. Dealing with reality is what the body-mind is profoundly good for. It is expressly designed for that.

And *that* is Peace. Ultimately, Peace is the open space, the availability, the receptiveness to *any* experience, including the experience of being unpeaceful. I know that might sound like word play, but the more we sit with this, the more it is realised that anything can arise. Nothing is in the mind's control. Anything can appear out there. Anything can appear in here. And what we are is simply responding to that. That is all. That is all it is. Over and over and over again, every minute.

That understanding makes it possible for the lived experience of what we are to align to the truth of what we are. The conscious mind shifts from believed controller to the witnesser, from the unquestioned authority to the space in which all narration arises.

The lived experience that we are not Peace is the only veil over the Peace that we really are. We are Intelligence in action. We are the awareness containing everything that arises. We are Aliveness of being animating all senses.

This understanding is sanity and it is incredible how capacity expands with that sanity, with that inherent knowing of Peace, of what we are. Because nothing is then ruled out. There is nothing to fear. There are no self-fulfilling prophesies of what is going to happen and how I'm going to feel. There is just what is, and there is the response to it. Over and over again. This is what life becomes: the simple meeting of what is there to be met from the truth of imperturbable (as the great Rupert Spira describes it) Peace of our being.

Capacity expands with the possibility now of experiencing discomfort. When we believed we had to look for Peace, that we had to somehow fix it in place, discomfort was unbearable. And so we would withdraw from anything that challenged the state of mind, the emotional status quo, the identity in which we believe we exist.

Now though, discomfort takes on a whole new possibility. It is an invitation to the edges of the comfort zone to see what is really true. And what is discovered in these edges is that concepts of ourselves, others and the world that were built from learnings of insecurity, risk, and conflict and which were held in place by resistance, fear and shame - are not the the reality we believed them to be.

The reality of self, other and the world is changing with each moment of presence to discomfort.

And now, the discomfort is welcomed in.

Welcomed in because it signifies that something infinitely more real and true is being revealed.

HOW PEACE IS VEILED

Peace comes from within. Do not seek it without.
Siddhārtha Gautama

*I*n stark contrast to my peaceful experience with the emotional roller coaster of IVF, is my decades long fear of public speaking.

I think it began aged about six when, dressed as a witch in a school Hallowe'en play I said 'cast a smell' instead of 'cast a spell'. All the kids fell about laughing as did the parents and teachers.

Well that's my memory of it. And it seemed to set the scene for on-going abject terror of speaking in any group larger than one, of being singled out in class. Anything that put a spot light on me was devastating.

I even blushed and grew tense at school when anyone I knew was called up to the front in assembly because somehow I felt that put attention on me too.

The emotions with it were absolutely awful, torture. I couldn't bear the feeling of dread, fear, shame, humiliation.

Unlike with the IVF, there was nothing saying, 'This isn't real. This is just chemistry, biology'. It looked personal, concretely real. I would do absolutely anything to get rid of the dreadful feelings and the only way I knew how to do that was to avoid anything that involved attention.

What was the difference?

Why could the roller coaster emotions of IVF be so peacefully accepted while avoiding the fear, tension and shame of public speaking occupied my every waking hour.

I have emails every day from people who are desperate to get rid of or change their experiences. The anxiety, the fear, the depression, the feelings of being limited, lacking, unloved, broken. *Of course* we want them gone. This state of lived resistance and tension is not how our system is designed to be. And we know that the more desperate we are to change something the more it seems to be fixed in place.

So, what is happening? If what we are is Peace, then why is our lived experience often so unpeaceful?

We are Consciousness, Aliveness or Intelligence momentarily located in transient, perception-created *form*.

The human form - the mind-brain-body or 'system' as I sometimes refer to it - has several requirements to flourish. Oxygen, hydration, shelter, a certain temperature range, nourishment, physical movement, social interaction, close relationships and meaningful activity.

From the cries of a new born onwards, actions are taken to meet these needs. That is the wiring of being human.

And in this respect we are not so different from any plant or animal. Plants growing towards or away from the sun. Cats hunting their prey. Chimpanzees with their complex social order.

The difference for us is two-fold:

Firstly, the human capacity for identification. We identify ourselves as being the temporary, separate, perception created form rather than living as the absolute and infinite which gives rise to that form.

Secondly, the human capacity for belief and conceptualisation. Once identification as a separate individual occurs it is cemented in place through layer upon layer of belief and through a developing concept of ourselves.

Identification, believing and conceptualisation are not bad things. In fact they are super-powers of a highly social species. They support integration, cohesion, familiarity, networks, travel, creativity, communication and language.

But, when they start to run the show, when they are taken as unquestioned reality, problems begin.

The truth of ourselves as being the infinite and absolute located in a body-mind that believes and acts according to what makes sense is forgotten.

And what starts to take up residence is that we are a separate individual self that can or should be controlling all elements of experience.

For some of us, as children, the idea of who and what we are, is created within an environment that is insecure, dangerous even.

We might have been surrounded by people who themselves were deeply confused about what they were and whose behaviour was unstable and unsafe. This developing self idea can be created in an environment of extreme lack and instability.

From that belief structure, from that trauma, from that sense of ourselves as not right, life is lived and the world is perceived.

All the time we are trying to get back to that knowing of what we were before this belief structure was created. We are trying to find Home. We are trying to return to the bliss of knowing ourselves as the infinite and absolute but we are trying to find it in the relative and the separate.

The human conscious mind, instead of residing in the infinite Consciousness of our true nature is now fully identified with the form.

An identified mind can only look for Peace through the conditional, through the belief in separation, through the belief in lack, control, and free-will, through the idea that there is something needed to attain Wholeness.

It looks like we are the body, the experience, the beliefs, the thoughts, the family, the job, the sports team, the street, the town, the country, the political party…

And it looks like Peace (which has now become synonymous with survival) will be found there.

We believe that by controlling emotions, controlling experience, controlling other people, controlling our circumstances we will be peaceful. It looks like Peace is a state that we will attain.

But the more we try to control these things, particularly emotions and experiences, the more 'unpeaceful' we become, because even in the moment of the right experience - "I'm happy now, I'm peaceful now, everything's exactly as it should be" we cannot, from this conditional space, truly be peaceful. We cannot feel at Peace because that attained moment of apparent Peace contains in it (of course it does) the certainty that it can not continue like that.

Any moment of everything being how we need it to be is inherently transient, fragile. It is already disappearing even as it appears.

We are either struggling to get the 'right' experience or clinging on to it when it appears, living the inevitability of the next bad emotion, the next bad experience, the next rejection, the next disaster…

The search for Peace is profoundly unpeaceful. No-one tells us this, so we don't know it. We are brought up thinking it is something to attain.

We look at other people – Yogis, or Guru's or billionaires or people who have what we think represents Peace and we envy them. We compare our own turbulent seas to their smooth sailing.

And first off, already, we are living a projection of our own beliefs: because we have no idea what's going on in people's minds and lives from moment to moment.

Then the thought becomes: "How do I get that?". That very thought "How do I get that?" is unpeaceful. While it continues and gathers more energy, the more unpeaceful we become and the mind begins to spiral. The more we try to find Peace, the more unpeaceful the mind, the more necessary the search seems and on and on…

This spiralling search for Peace is at the heart of our mental health crisis. It is a very natural, very understandable attempt to find Peace – because we know it, we had it as a baby, we know what we are. But the misunderstanding of Peace is the problem. The more we try to find it, the more unpeaceful our experience, the more it looks like there's something wrong with us, the more we try different pills and medicines and distractions and drugs and anything else that will numb that inner space. The whole experience of being snow-balls into unrest, vigilance and control.

All of this is done in an attempt to find the space that we know is our birthright. Yet all of it obscures the Peace we already are.

HOW PEACE IS REVEALED

If you are willing to experience anything directly and immediately, whether good or bad, joyous or hateful, you will recognise that what you are running from does not exist, and what you are running toward is already here.
Gangaji

The public speaking phobia continued through different jobs and roles. I scraped through the presentations I had to do feeling absolutely sick.

At the same time I continued exploring what the mind is, what reality is, what the idea of ourselves is.

One day, I knew I was going to do a talk in my house for a small group of friends. The thought came in with dreadful inevitability. I felt sick at the idea of it and yet I knew it was going to happen. The same tensions arose but this time something was different.

The tension, fear and apprehension were there but this time the experience of them was almost irrelevant. The same future projections crowded in - me losing my voice, shaking so much I couldn't stand up, walking out, being sick - but this time even if they came true there was a sense that it wouldn't matter.

The life and death nature of the phobia had gone.

And the only reason for the fear no longer looking like survival is that it had become obvious that it wasn't, actually, about survival.

The 'I' identified with self image, control, resistance and seeking was dissolving. And its dissolution was revealing what couldn't be touched no matter what the experience.

Understanding stress or discomfort isn't as simple as telling ourselves 'it's just my thinking'. It is not the case that we can just paint over experience with clever spiritual words and have the whole thing sorted out as if by magic.

There are stressors that are humanity-wide (eg. violence, poverty, captivity, discrimination, hunger, thirst, sleep, temperature…). There are variables that which, when not right for the individual, can also create stress (eg. noise, stimulation, contact, pressure…).

We must not use a conversation about reality to deny the drive (and right) of the 'body-mind system' to find its optimum, nourished, thriving and balanced status.

And yet, this conversation about reality, self, the mind and experience, presents a conundrum when it comes to Peace…

Because the human mind, in all its infinite creativity, has a capacity, tendency even, to project its own insecurities, shame and fears and then react to this projection with stress and tension as though the projection is reality.

We see this in ourselves all the time. When we are low or tired, tasks seem harder. When we are insecure, other people seem more indifferent or superior. When we are anxious, our environment seems harsher and more dangerous. When we are ashamed, the world seems to judge us.

And this of course is a vicious circle.

The harder the tasks appear, the more tired we feel and the harder the tasks look.

The more superior others appear, the more insecure we feel and the more confident others appear.

And so on…

What this reveals is that the self is not separate from the tasks, other people, environment or the world. It is all made of understanding, belief, thought in that moment.

What do we do about that?

How do we make sure we acknowledge the 'real' stressors that will not disappear no matter how settled the mind?

How do we know what to honour and orientate towards or away from in a reality that, to a great extent, is mind created?

It is quite a conundrum.

And one which cannot be adequately addressed by either taking reality at unquestioned face value or, alternatively, denying all reality.

So where to begin?

It begins with what question we are asking ourselves.

'How can I get rid of stress and find Peace?' does not take us even slightly far enough. It leaves us at the level of addressing symptoms without understanding what gave rise to them.

We need a question that creates the space for both current experience, for exploration of what is true and for the system to find its right way to be.

A more powerful question therefore might be…

'Where is freedom?'

This question takes us to the freedom of the body to express its 'dis-ease'…

the freedom to honour the current experience…

the freedom that is veiled by the limited believed idea of what we are, of what we have to do, of how we have to live and which is revealed as that idea loses its grip…

the freedom for changes to be made, 'yes' or 'no' to be said, harm to be prevented, desire and needs to be expressed…

the freedom of life aligned, expressed, balanced and nourished in that individual…

And, ultimately, the freedom to bring this about for all seven billion of us humans, plus the rest of the planet.

How is that freedom revealed? How does the body-mind system align to its ultimate truth of Peace to end the cycle of creating and fighting projections.

There are several ways back in. One of them, which is not necessary by any means is hitting rock bottom. Many teachers have described a feeling of being at their absolute lowest, where there's nowhere else to go, when there's the realisation of the absolute futility of what the mind had been trying to do, that literally there are no answers in that struggle.

There is not the slightest hope, or glimpse of truth, in that desperation, in that self-loathing, in that helplessness. There is nothing there. Someone hits rock bottom and in that space, there is nothing left. It is as if everything has gone and all that remains in that space *is* Aliveness, *is* Consciousness, *is* Intelligence. That is it. Everything else has gone and it becomes, in that moment, the only thing that we are.

So that *does* happen. It makes total sense that that happens. And... it is not necessary. It is not necessary for everything to collapse around us, because that same orientation that happens when there's nothing left can happen at any time. It simply comes from a different understanding of what is true.

Earlier in HOME we considered the significance of a glimpse, or a moment of realisation. It might not come as an insight, or a clearing or a space. It might be that there's just a moment of engagement in a task for example. Or a moment looking up at a night sky or the sunset or sunrise or a mountain range or an animal – that sense of wonder or marvel.

These are the things we can start to see are true. These are the things that get so overlooked: that sense of flow, that opening to marvel, that space of just pure presence. That is what we are.

While the search for Peace, the search for control, the search for a different experience of what we are, that is the 'untruth'. That is the insanity.

Before it looked as though the search would secure Peace. Now it becomes clear that it is the very thing that hides the Peace that we are.

The whole body now, the whole mind, everything in the brain, is starting to orientate now to this moment-by-moment response. Intelligence is meeting reality.

And the body-mind, the response and the external reality that is being responded to, have less and less gaps between them. Living is one seamless fluidity. That is the mind settling back into its truth.

That is the Peace of being Home.

IN SUMMARY...

Peace

WHAT IS IT?

The imperturbable nature of existence that remains untouched no matter the experience.

Openness to all experience.

WHAT VEILS IT?

The belief that we are something other than intelligence in action.

The attempt to control experience, emotions, the mind, thoughts and beliefs in order to be peaceful.

The attempt to ignore or deny the needs of the mind-body to flourish.

. . .

What reveals it?

The realisation that existence will remain regardless of all experience.

PART VII
LOVE

Should you really open your eyes and see, you would behold your image in all images. And should you open your ears and listen, you would hear your own voice in all voices.
Khalil Gibran

Once upon a time there was an old man standing at a grave clutching a bunch of flowers. The man's wife had died. They had been everything for each other and now he felt completely alone.

The man bent down to lay the flowers on the grave. As he did so a small dog ran up to him and started licking his hand.

The man picked the dog up and looked around for its owner. There was no one in the Church yard. He looked for a collar. No collar or identification to be found.

'What to do?' wondered the man. 'Maybe I should leave him here to find his way home'. So he put the dog back down and started to walk away.

The dog followed him.

The man picked the dog up and returned him to the grave yard.

When he left, the dog followed him.

After five such attempts, the man gave up trying to send the dog away.

When he got home, he made some calls to local vets, to the RSPCA, to the police even to see if anyone had reported a lost dog. He wrote out posters and pinned them to lampposts near the grave yard with his phone number and the dog's description.

There was no response. No one had reported a missing dog. And so the dog stayed.

The man enjoyed the dog's company more and more every day. The dog gave him new purpose and interest. In the mornings instead of being unable to get up and face the day, he was downstairs in his pyjamas making breakfast for them both. On his walks, people stopped to pat the dog and conversations started up. When he was sad, the dog would be there, snuggling into his arms. In the evenings, the dog would curl up on his feet. He would look into the dog's eyes and see such open trust. He felt himself becoming worthy of that regard.

Several years of beautiful companionship went past, then one day, the man noticed that the dog was whimpering and more tired than usual.

The man hoped the dog would get better with some rest and care but the pain seemed to get worse.

The man took the dog to the vet. By then the dog's eyes were closing. There was something very wrong.

The vet gave his diagnosis saying, "I'm sorry sir. This is inoperable and there is too much pain."

This was the worst news possible for the man. He staggered, his legs weak under the weight of the words.

He held the dog tightly against his chest, this dog that had opened up his world. This dog that he loved with all his heart.

He could not imagine what his life would be like. He wanted to cling on to the dog. Keep it alive. He desperately wanted to run from the surgery, take the dog home. Even just for another few days… another hour.

He looked at the vet through eyes blurred with tears. There was no question.

'Yes.' he said, holding out his arms, allowing the dog to be taken from him.

'Of course.'

WE ARE LOVE

The fundamental nature of Infinite Intelligence is unity and love. It responds to all your thoughts as if they were moving toward love. This is why your subconscious mind will bring forth whatever thought, plan, or idea you impress upon it, good or bad. It will embrace every thought with love and bring it forth.
Joseph Murphy

Any pet owner who has put to sleep a suffering pet that they adore with all their heart knows implicitly everything that this chapter could ever say. Or far less common but even more heart-wrenching, to turn off the machines supporting the life of a loved one when no other possibility remains.

You could close this book now. You know everything.

You know what it is to remain in and act from the most open, sane, unconditional, present, loving truth of your being even while everything on the surface is distraught and in protest and desperately wanting the opposite of what you know you must do.

This is unconditional love in action. It shows the incredible capacity, courage, selflessness and compassion that is possible when behaviour comes from the truth of our nature.

By terrible contrast, consider a tragic event unfolding in the news as I write this. A father writes a note to his wife before killing his three children and then killing himself. The note said, "If I can't be happy, why should you?'

The hatred, control, insanity and vindictiveness to create such horror even from beyond the grave shows how utterly obscured our true nature of unconditional love can become and the indescribable harm and suffering that is created as a result.

If you spend anytime with different spiritual teachers you will see that there are many things that they don't agree on.

Consciousness, Intelligence, wisdom, non-duality, nothing-ness, being-ness, formless, form, ego, spirituality, the 'Three Principles', reality... all of that is debated. Different teachers have different ways of talking about them. Some denying the existence truth or relevance of them. Some saying this is all there is.

Yet, they all, every single one, agree that the ultimate truth of our being is unconditional Love.

Unanimous.

And when they talk about it, there is a pervasive simplicity, joy and peacefulness that you can't help feeling from the other side of the room, screen or book.

This is why this is the last 'pointing' of the book.

What is this force that unites all teaching?

What is unconditional Love?

It's impossible to define it. How could we?

We could say that it is the combination of everything we have considered in this book: pure presence, perfect organising Intelligence, the juiciness of being, completeness and undisturbable Peace.

All of this wrapped up in the utter kindness of the design. A design that continually brings the mind Home.

It often doesn't seem, though, that the design is kind. When the mind is fighting its own creations. When the concept of self and other lies heavily. The more the thoughts get stuck revolving in this idea of me as vulnerable, a victim, hard done by, isolated, separate, then in those moments the world is unkind, there is no Love. It's a harsh unkind world. And in those moments, *I* am not Love; other people are not Love; other people are out to get me, or ignore me, they don't care. The resistant mind can never experience beingness as unconditional Love. It can't because resistance is only about conditions.

But in those moments of no resistance... in the moments of no mind really.... and these moments might even happen when the circumstances are absolutely dire... there might just be the purest experience of being. A moment in which everything, everyone in that moment is lit up by Love. It comes from a falling away of the idea that it should be anything else but this.

Even in the most intense anxiety or depression, the deepest grief, the most thudding rejection there is a glow of light. And that light is Love.

That light is not hope. It is not the idea that everything will be alright.

The light is presence to this right now. This is all there is and this is Love. The kindness of the design is that it allows for a mind that can create anything, that can get utterly lost fighting its own reflection to find its way home. The way Home is illuminated in the suffering.

Even just a slight shift or reorientation in relation to what we are, to what the world is, starts to make the distinction between the transient and the permanent. Every interaction highlights the shift between conditions and the unconditional. Between the relative and the absolute.

It becomes clear that the mind identified with individuality in this moment is hiding the inner unconditional depth of being, the unconditional being that we really are. This is an incredible new orientation. It turns life in this form into an on-going revelation of the Love that we are. It starts to be revealed everywhere, in every moment.

We could say enlightenment ultimately is the dissolution of those veils hiding the Love that we are. Layers dissolving until all that remains is Love in a temporary, subjective, apparent form seeing itself everywhere. In every person, in every tree, in every animal, in every circumstance. Everywhere.

The battle to control a situation or change a person or to get enough attention and validation that we feel we are loved is over.

Knowing ourselves as unconditional Love is simultaneously the hardest and the easiest shift. It is, at the same time, the most obscure and the most obvious, the most confronting and the most deeply known within our being.

All of us will have had moments of everything falling away. Depending on the grip of the mind and identification they may be so fleeting as to be unnoticed. It might be a moment of looking into someone's eyes and seeing right through the barriers, seeing the Love that we are in them. It might be in nature or looking up at the night sky. It's an alive electric space of Love, however fleeting, however unbelievable for the mind.

The appearance of separation and the feeling of isolation it inevitably brings can take the body-mind system deeper into its confusion.

Or this suffering is seen for what it is: an indication of the insanity of mind, of delusion, of lostness.

Because suffering IS the way back to the unconditional space of no requirements, no resistance, no resentment, no self, no other. Just this.

It is empty of content because content has no truth. And this emptiness is bliss. It is not the harsh bleak nihilistic emptiness that a mind fully lost in separation will create. It is empty, warm, vibrant alive no-thing.

The rediscovering, or the return of the mind back Home is unconditional Love in action. From that truth, the mind and body can move back into the world. And now the world does not have to change for us to be ok. There are no conditions imposed on other people. And ironically this is the only space of change. The mind is no longer in battle with its own projected beliefs. There is just absolute intimacy with what is.

The entire purpose of our lives is our return to the knowing of ourselves as unconditional Love.

And this is done through the people who have hurt us most, whose behaviour, whose words to us, whose actions towards us largely created and reinforced that sense of lack, that fragility of self identity.

This is a return back through these layers to the truth of Wholeness and to the truth of unconditional Love in which even the people who have done the worst things to us are understood. Their behaviour could not have been any different. Their behaviour, no matter how terrible, came from their own search for Wholeness, from their own desperation to return to Love.

This is beyond forgiveness. It is a place in which all conditions have fallen away. It is a meeting of the other and ourselves in the full knowledge that there is no decider. There is only a search for Home or a knowing of Home.

Our life, every interaction, every relationship in which we are seeking Love, in which we are trying to *be* loved, so that we can be whole, so that we can be at Peace, is saying "No. It is not out here. There will never be enough out here to make you whole. From that perspective of lack, you cannot ever find Wholeness".

In every interaction when we are desperate for Love, desperate for recognition, to be held by someone, the kindness of the design is saying "No, not there. Come back, come back, come back, come back. Come back to that glow, that tiny, alive, vibrant sliver of unconditional Love that is truth and is freedom and go out from there. "

From truth, everything is Love.

Unconditionally.

Unanimously.

HOW LOVE IS VEILED

If I ever go looking for my heart's desire again, I won't look any further than my own back yard. Because if it isn't there, I never really lost it to begin with.
Noel Langley, The Wizard of Oz

In the American version of The Office, two characters Ryan and Kelly have an office romance and after a while it ends. Ryan, reflecting on their relationship post break-up, says of Kelly *'I'd rather she be alone than with someone else... Is that love...?'*

An alien researching the definition of human love according to popular culture might well agree with him.

'Absolutely Ryan,' it would say in its alien voice. 'You are spot on. Love on Planet Earth in the 21st century is entirely about how the other person makes us feel and what they have to do or not do to maintain that.'

It reminds me of a postcard I saw years ago which said,

'If you love something, set it free. If it doesn't come back, hunt it down and kill it.'

On one level this is humorous. On another level it points to the very worst of our actions when it looks like our salvation will be found through the control of another.

Our soap operas, romances, movies, novels and songs tell us what Love is. Possession. Control. Inter-dependency. Need. Desire. Indifference. Revenge. Completion and Wholeness through another. Almost unanimously, they tell us that Love is all there is. *And* that, for Love to be realised, we need to be loved.

And that sets up quite a task.

Because it is true, ultimately Love IS all there is. It IS the sense of being home, of being settled, of being complete, of the un-altering foundation from which to live life.

But... other people are not necessarily the most reliable places on which to pin the stability of our entire existence.

They don't always do what we want them to.

Sometimes they prefer to hang out with other people rather than us.

They have their own needs and wants that can conflict with ours.

They might ghost us. They might leave us. They might die.

The attempt to realise Love can be so confusing, so veiled, so confronting.

The word Love has been completely taken and claimed by the conditional, by a world of romantic love, familial love,

love of our pets or our surroundings. It's claimed by the objective: it is a love *of* something or a love *from* someone. It looks like it depends on the behaviour of someone to us, how we're perceived, the regard that we're held in.

Love is perhaps the ultimate blurred space in a conversation about what we are.

The knowing of our true nature as unconditional Love does not stop the body-mind from delighting in family, friendship, romance and sex. On the contrary, this knowing space is the *only* place in which those relationships can genuinely flourish.

But to use these relationships to *find* our true nature and, in the attempt, to end the suffering of separation is where confusion lies.

The self identity arose in that blurred space between the survival of the physical and the survival of the idea of me. Our relationships and the people around us while the self identity is forming create a blue print of separation between the self and another. This blue print becomes the lens of lack through which the world is viewed.

Love looks to be the way in which we can return to that remembered space of Wholeness before the idea of separation arose.

The desire to stabilise what we are, to be whole, to be someone or something looks like it is related to Love, somehow.

This *is* true in the sense that the ultimate stability is the recognition that we *are* Love. But the conditioning of lack sends us out to try and find our Wholeness from a fractured place and the only outcome is more fracture.

It looks like the way to remedy this lack is to find the thing that will make us whole, to be loved enough and then we'll be all right.

But this search to be loved enough that we become whole is a wild goose chase because it is the search, the looking out there that veils the fact that we are Love already.

And the terrible irony of all of this is that the more necessary it looks to us that Love has to be found 'out there' the harder we try to find it, the more life is a series of rejections and knock backs.

And this is because the appearance of reality is a projection from the inside. These rejections are our own conditioning of lack and incompleteness reflected back over and over again. Each time, saying the same message 'You are Love already. It cannot be found out here. Realise Love first and then go from there.'

And from there, what happens?

Maybe we could go back to Ryan for the answer and the last words of this chapter.

The interviewer asks a now more grounded Ryan about his relationship with Kelly and he looks to the camera and says simply...

'I can't explain it'.

HOW LOVE IS REVEALED

The ultimate love is the mind's love of itself. Mind joins with mind —all of mind, without division or separation, all of it loved. Ultimately I am all I can know, and what I come to know is that there is no such thing as 'I.'
Byron Katie

The return to school was the hardest. I didn't know how to be with people again and people didn't know how to be with me. My teacher, a stern ex-army sergeant, made no reference to where I'd been. In the playground, a friend asked me 'Are you happy?' I replied yes and she said 'You shouldn't be. Your Daddy has died.' I stayed there for a moment trying to be OK but then...

It's hard to be ten and to lose the gentlest, funniest, most intelligent father imaginable. It's hard to be any age and lose anyone you love. And when we say 'hard' we can of course mean anything from upsetting to beyond devastating.

Everything in the human life drives us to closeness with others. The family unit as we are growing up, the reliance on the mother and father, the siblings and extended family. Then the making of friends, the finding of a partner perhaps, the settling down, the having of our own children or caring for those of others. The orientation of human being is the formation of strong bonds. (With consequences for all of us when these bonds are not formed, trusted or are broken or dangerous.)

Which means that we live in these close bonds with the possibility of losing the people that mean most to us, who we speak to every day or spend most of our time with, who know our deepest secrets, who have our backs, who we love with all our hearts.

How can we live with the possibility of the loss of these most precious beings and how can we live with that loss if it happens?

How can the love we have for others reveal the Love at the centre of our being. A Love that places no conditions on any other. Not even that they stay alive.

This must be the greatest conundrum of human relationships. In the words of the brilliant Mary Oliver:

"To live in this world, you must be able to do three things: to love what is mortal; to hold it against your bones knowing your own life depends on it; and, when the time comes to let it go, to let it go."

How to do that?

We could start with a video with Byron Katie talking to a woman whose daughter died in a car crash. They had been driving in two different cars on the motorway. Her daughter had been in the car behind and the mother saw the fatal accident happen. The woman's life had become a living hell. She no longer lived but barely existed. Everything reminded her of her daughter and in particular everything brought to mind the scene of the crash. She could not bear her memories. She could not bear to be in her head. Everything was intolerable. Her existence had become a constant fight against what happened, against the unfairness, against her thoughts.

Byron Katie with the gentlest, unwavering kindness showed her that anything that isn't now is a creation of the mind. Even when someone is in the room next to us they only exist, in that moment, in imagination. Even when someone is right next to us, everything about the way they appear is appearing through the filters of perception.

Again and again we come back to what the mind creates. How you appear to me is my version of you. The only relation it has to your version of you or anyone else's version of you is if our minds have had similar conditioning, learned the same beliefs, associations and distortions. The greater the disparity in culture, societal rules, the less similar will be our versions of each other.

In other words, we exist for each other as creations of our own (largely) unconscious mind. And the wonderful, beautiful, extraordinary thing is that, as this becomes clear, it doesn't take away the other. No. It delivers them to us more fully, more vividly, more expansively than we could ever imagine.

The irony is that, the more clearly it is seen that there is no other, the more absolute freedom there is to know and to love that other with every fibre of our being.

And let's illustrate this with an example from the other extreme.

Because you might be thinking, 'Well, that's all very well to say about the people we love already. But what about the people who have done us real harm? The manipulators, abusers, the rapists, the violent? The supposed care-givers and bullies who turned our childhoods into a living hell. What about them?

And for this, thankfully, we have the astonishing leadership of Dr Edith Eger, a psychologist and expert in post traumatic stress disorder who was imprisoned in Auschwitz and other camps. Her parents and fiancé were killed in the gas chambers. She and her sister barely survived 'the death march' to the Gunskirchen concentration camp.

Towards the end of her masterpiece, *'The Choice'*, she describes a client, a fourteen year old boy, coming into her office, sitting in her chair and saying, "It's time for America to be white again. I'm going to kill all the Jews, all the niggers, all the Mexicans, all the chinks."

Can you imagine?

After everything she had endured. Her initial reaction of course was blind outrage and anger. She felt sick. She felt hatred. She wanted to get as far away from him as possible.

And yet an instruction came to her. An instruction that is almost unfathomable given her experience of abject cruelty and a life dedicated to the end of prejudice.

The instruction said, 'Find the bigot in you. Find the part in you that is judging, assigning labels, diminishing another's humanity, making others less than who they are.'

And she did it.

She found the place where she and the boy were the same and she came to the realisation,

"I had an opportunity to love this young person, just for him, for his singular being and our shared humanity. The opportunity to welcome him to say anything, feel any feeling, without the fear of being judged."

The enormity of this is beyond words. This is transcendence. This is the realisation of unconditional Love.

Understanding the mind, understanding the role of conditioning, understanding that our self identity cannot ever be secured by another or by resisting another is to live in this moment right now.

And then we really see them. As they are.

Not as the solution to our needs and insecurities.

Not as the object of our dependencies.

Not as the villain, the source of our issues and frustrations.

Not as a victim, the evidence of our evil.

Not as someone to change or fix so that we can feel better.

Not as the guarantor of our future or the preserver of our past.

Not as something that has to be held on to, sought out or resisted.

But as what they really are. As what we really are.

Life localised in apparent, perception-created, conditioning-shaped, unique, miraculous form. The same as us.

And from this space we see the loss of them or the presence of them as it really is:

The dissolution of that unique apparent form but the continuation of it… in the only place it ever really existed… in us, our mind, our life, our actions, our words.

They live in us. They are us.

We are Love. It is impossible that the other is any different from us. It is impossible that they exist outside of the mind's creation of them. Everything about that mind's creation will change and shift in line with the revelation of ourselves as unconditional Love.

This is a space of freedom in which we don't even have to forgive other people, there was no one doing the behaviour. There is no one to forgive. All behaviour is only ever the attempt to return back to the Love we are.

How can it be anything but unconditional Love that allows the body-mind to think anything it thinks and feel anything it feels? The identified mind rails against this liberty of expression as it craves the control of only experiencing certain things

But now the body-mind is aligning to the unconditional.

To the meeting of whatever is there to be met.

The shift is away from the search, from the attempt to stabilise what cannot be stabilised, towards the simple recognition of what doesn't change.

And every cell in the body settles into that vital, inner glowing perfection that we always have been.

The feeling of being separate from this is saying, return to what's true. This. Now. This. Have all of it. Live all of it.

Unconditionally.

Live it until you know it can never be lost.

IN SUMMARY...

Love

WHAT IS IT?

The utter kindness, bliss and joy of being.

The perfection of life in form.

Unconditional freedom.

WHAT VEILS IT?

The attempt to experience our true nature of unconditional love through manipulating or controlling others.

Looking for the absolute of love in the relative form.

. . .

What reveals it?

The realisation that all others are the mirrors of us.

The suffering when we feel separate from another.

PART VIII
CONCLUSION

In the same way that a glass of water is exponentially more satisfying after a five-mile hike in the desert, the experience of feeling the interconnectedness of everything is more fulfilling after the illusion of separation. This is the fun of the game. This is the fun of waking up.
Chris Niebauer

NOTHING TO BE GAINED

The dilemma for the individual is not that the individual can't get what it wants - the dilemma is apparent individuality.
Tony Parsons

I was on a non-duality retreat and the teacher began by standing up and saying "There is no point in your being here……It doesn't matter if you come to any of the talks. There is nothing whatsoever to be gained. You might as well be outside in the gardens or in your room."

There is absolute honesty in this because it is true that there is nothing for the self identity or ego to be gained – ever. The ego which is essentially the search for Peace, freedom and joy is obscuring the Peace, freedom and joy of the life we are already. Before, during, after the retreat… no difference.

The teacher knew this – hence the words.

The end of the seeking comes with the realisation that there is nothing to be found, that there is no seeker even. This is the constant pointing of all non-duality and spiritual teaching from the very ancient to the modern:

What we are looking for is here already.

It is the search for it that obscures it.

It is the idea of ourself as separate, as needing something to secure that self idea, that hides the Wholeness of being that is all there is.

It is this search that is the only confusion.

'There is nothing whatsoever to be gained' these words are coming from someone who clearly has realised them. The teacher spoke his words with love. The teacher was happy, smiling, making jokes, laughing, eyes sparkling. The teacher had strong relationships with his partner, family and friends. The teacher teaches and writes books and does other expressive activities. The teacher is healthy, vital and vibrant in his body.

The teacher wasn't isolated in his house afraid to leave because of panic attacks and anxiety. The teacher wasn't trapped in his bed by a sense of inadequacy or worthlessness, unable to get up and start the day. The teacher wasn't self-harming or abusing others or numbing away painful thoughts with drink or drugs. The teacher was profoundly present in the room, no anger at the past or terror at the future. And although there was plenty of disagreement and correcting of what the students said, there was no conflict with anything or anyone. And there was laughter. So much beautiful laughter.

It is the falling away of the idea of self, it is the end of the search for happiness, Peace and freedom that brings everything into thriving alignment.

And this is the paradox with the realisation of Home.

Until there is the realisation that there is nothing to realise, that Home is where we are already, there can be suffering. Often significant suffering. Often torturous suffering. Misunderstood suffering that sets up its own vicious circle in the scrambling for relief. Even though, as many teachers say, 'nothing is happening to no one', the experience of being away from Home can create intense despair, depression, hopelessness, conflict, anxiety and harm to self and others.

So how to address the suffering that comes with the insecurity of believing ourselves to be separate from life, from Intelligence without continuing and exacerbating the wild goose chase to secure that non-existent individuality?

Many teachers say we don't need to, that it is not real, there is no one suffering and that any attempt to alleviate the suffering is only reinforcing the ego-self. But is that just to leave someone lost in the suffering the mind creates?

Let's imagine a river.

On one side is the student, suffering, desperate and miserable, shouting across to the teacher, 'How do I cross the river? How do I get to the other side?'

And on the one side is the teacher saying over and over again, 'There is no side to get to. There is no river. There is nothing to do and nowhere to get to. There is no river.'

But as long as the student's mind is lost in itself then the river looks absolutely real. It looks to the student that there is a difference between them and the teacher, that there is a gulf between them and the Peace, happiness, freedom and Love they are searching for. It looks like there is somewhere to get to, a river to cross and as long as it looks like there is a river to cross then the search is obscuring the truth.

So, what to do?

How can that student be supported without increasing the search?

How does the search end?

What we are really asking is:

Where does the realisation that 'there is absolutely nothing to attain' come from?

How does the seeking, restless, insecure mind settle into simply being?

How does it become so obvious that we are Home that the attempt to get there becomes absolutely ridiculous?

Are we really saying there is nothing we can do to help this happen?

I don't think so. Even the teacher that is saying, 'Don't stay in this conversation. There is nothing to gain.' is apparently holding the retreat and writing the books. And the retreats and the books are agents of realisation and confirmation of truth. If they weren't, they wouldn't be attended or read.

Because until these questions are answered, there is something to be realised. There are veils obscuring the truth of what we are. And those veils, entirely insubstantial as they are, made of nothing, thoughts, wisps of air, are also blocks of concrete.

From what I have seen over my courses and programmes, enormous changes occur when the mind shifts out of identification with its own story of separation and resentment.

When that frantic whirring activity of resistance and seeking settles it reveals the presence that was there all along.

True sanity, the sanity of Intelligence responding to reality is unveiled.

There is an intimacy with the present moment and all it contains, there is learning, honesty and openness that were not possible in the resistance and attempt to control.

The body, previously held in the tension of the on-going fight and flight reaction, relaxes. Stress-related diseases disappear.

There are ways – many ways – in which the realisation of true nature and, with that, a dramatic reduction in how suffering is misunderstood – can be brought about without creating more confusion.

In this book we only have one option available: conscious enquiry into the nature of thought, belief, concepts and reality. There is beautiful logic and rationality in this exploration that a curious mind can engage in. Every shift in understanding is a dissolution of the beliefs holding believed separation in place.

Other elements in my courses are:

Above all, love and support (because this conversation is death to the identity and its desperation for control. Feeling safe enough for that tightest of grips to loosen can be everything)

Equally above all, a focus on the body (to allow the sensations that have been long repressed, to heal, nurture and respect what might have long been neglected, to bring attention back to the closest we have to reality)

Supported observation of our own words, actions and reactions (to make transparent how the conditioning of separation is being maintained, to carry out this exploration in honesty, openness, humility and accountability)

Subliminal support (to amplify what is subconsciously known about our true nature)

Supported, courageous presence to experiences that trigger shame, insecurity, fear and need (to feel whatever is there to be felt, to expand beyond the imprisoning concepts, to see that through these experiences lies a whole other reality of self and other)

In making that shift from identification to presence, we reverse the process in which that insecure identification was created in the first place. For those who have experienced trauma, neglect, violence or abuse, love and support are especially critical to allow the settling back into safety, into the reality of the physical.

Each step forward into the river represents a lightening of the burden of seeking, a falling away of what is not, or is no longer, true.

After each step, there is a look back to see how far we have come, only to realise that there is no river behind us. We have not crossed anything.

Yet there is still river ahead. Another step. Another look back and again no river behind us.

Until, lightening by lightening, dissolution by dissolution, step by step the river is crossed.

We are on the other side.

And it is clear there is no river.

It is clear there is no teacher.

We are in exactly the same place we were before.

Nothing has changed.

Nothing needed to be realised.

And yet… everything is completely different.

Home.

BREATHE, ALIGN, DEEPEN

Joy is a return to the deep harmony of body, mind, and spirit that was yours at birth and that can be yours again. That openness to love, that capacity for wholeness with the world around you, is still within you.
Deepak Chopra

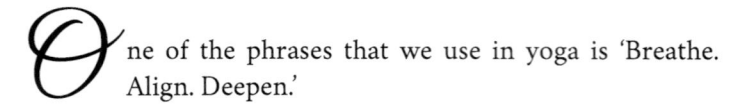

One of the phrases that we use in yoga is 'Breathe. Align. Deepen.'

Breathe – focus on the breath, this brings everything into this moment, a deep immersion in the body, in the pose, allowing the Intelligence of life that we are to respond to this what is, right now. Without that attention and presence, no yoga.

Align – align the body within the pose, get the basics of the pose right, come back to beginner stages and easier versions if the form is lost or if parts of the body are compensating for weaker areas

And only once there is presence to breath and a body moving in alignment with the pose, is it time to *Deepen* the practice – either through deeper stretches, more advanced versions or through lengthening the duration of the pose.

It is the mantra for the healthy and safe development of our yoga practice, it is also a mantra that we would do well to live by for healthy, safe and sane experience of ourselves and the world beyond the mat.

Let's look at how this works

Breathe – the route to presence, reality and therefore sanity

- Allow attention to come into reality, into the body, into the breath, into this moment. Notice suffering, tension, tightness and resistance.
- Feel what there is to be felt in every moment.
- Come into the physical sensations right now – these are the only access point to truth.
- Notice where the mind is, what it is creating, what projections are happening and how these have nothing to do with right now, that these creations are veiling the fact that there is only this
- A mind engaged with reality is sane and sanity is always the place to begin.

Align – the route to accountability, coherence and therefore stability

- Now attention can check in to see what is and is not consistent with truth
- Are our words and actions aligned to reality?
- Are our words and actions towards ourself (what we

eat and drink, how we move, how we treat ourselves, what we say to ourselves) aligned to the preciousness of life in form?
- How about our words and actions towards other people, are they aligned to the truth that there is no other?
- Or are they out of sync with what is true? Are we pretending, manipulating, lying, taking offence, defending, resenting, blaming, distancing, trying to control – all in order to protect a self concept that doesn't even exist?
- Until there is coherence between behaviour and truth, there is no point in doing or expanding, as all words and actions taken from misalignment amplify the problems we are trying to get rid of
- Alignment of behaviour with truth, presence and reality is ultimate accountability. It is the recognition of ourselves as the source and it is the dissolution of any sense of separation between self and other. This is the ultimate stability.

We could spend a lot of time between these two steps: breathe and align. That's OK. This is our life's work. This is our only purpose. On the mat, off the mat. In relationships, work, hobbies, money, creating, everything… Over and over again to return to what is true and for our actions and words to adjust accordingly.

Deepen – the expansion that comes automatically from sanity and stability

- Going deeper into life will happen easily and effortlessly though alignment.
- Alignment of words, actions, understanding to truth,

to reality will open up possibilities that previously could not even be seen, let alone attempted.
- Presence and congruency of every cell, every thought, every behaviour with truth means that desires already contain their fulfilment, every change wanted is already happening at source
- With each moment of presence and each alignment to that truth, there is a new sense of what we are and a new reality
- Every aspect of this new reality is built on the most robust of foundations: Consciousness, Intelligence, Aliveness, Wholeness, Peace and Love

bringing us back to where we already are.

HOME.

EPILOGUE

To travel a circle is to journey over the same ground time and time again. To travel a circle wisely is to journey over the same ground for the first time. In this way, the ordinary becomes extraordinary, and the circle, a path to where you wish to be. And when you notice at last that the path has circled back into itself, you realise that where you wish to be is where you have already been ... and always were.

Neale Donald Walsch

This is my seventh book and it has been, by far, the hardest to write.

I thought it would be easy but it turns out using words to describe what comes before words is not that straightforward. Who knew?

I hope there may have been at least parts that have resonated, that have spoken to what has always been known.

There is nothing new here. There is nothing that isn't known in your every cell.

There is nothing lacking. There is nowhere to get to. There is nothing to do.

Everything we have been looking for is here already.

And maybe… perhaps… the conscious mind, the experience of what we are, the body, the words and the actions can settle back into that truth.

It is time to go through the door that once was so familiar. Place our shoes in the hallway, keys in their usual place, maybe put the kettle on, sink into the comfiest chair, look around, smile at the deep remembering of it all.

Settled. Safe. Essential. Familiar. Sound. Right. Truthful. Known.

Home.

Coming back to what we had never left.

The return to what we already are.

Home.

Then, now, always.

ALSO BY CLARE DIMOND

There is an on-line 60 day course on which this book was based with recordings, subliminal recordings, webinars and conversations.

Details of how to join HOME and other on-line courses from Clare can be found here.

https://claredimond.com

Other books from Clare Dimond in the REAL series are:

REAL the inside-out guide to being yourself

FREE getting real with life unlimited

EASE getting real with work

GAME getting real with the play of life

SANE getting real with reality

WELL getting real with mental and physical health

Printed in Great Britain
by Amazon